"There continues to be discu: ʼs are burned out and/or leaving th‹ ›ook, Douglas Webster has put his ... ᴏ... ... .... .. ..., .. .entral factor: we have unknowingly adopted a model from Christendom that tends to isolate the pastor from the flock. Webster argues for a 'dynamic synergy' between pastoral identity and congregational identity, urging us to recapture the New Testament's emphasis on the role of every member in the body of Christ. His case is compelling, and greatly needed in the current climate. Webster's engagement with church history is especially illuminating about the nature of pastoral ministry, and his own pastoral experiences add to the book's credibility, wisdom, and practicality. I hope this helpful and important book will gain a wide readership!"

—Dr. Gavin Orlund,
Senior Pastor, First Baptist Church of Ojai (CA)

"With his characteristic and uncompromising accent on the priesthood of all believers, Doug Webster critiques the lingering image of the pastor from medieval Christendom to modern times. This thought-provoking pastoral theology will help alleviate unrealistic (and unbiblical) expectations that continue to crush the clergy and debilitate the laity. Even after many years in ministry, this book has challenged me to reconsider my own pastoral identity and practice. It has profoundly affected the way I train pastoral ministry students."

—Jason R. McConnell,
Senior Pastor, Franklin United Church, Franklin, VT;
Adjunct Professor of Pastoral Ministry,
Gordon-Conwell Theological Seminary

"After twenty years of ordained ministry in a mainline church, I can attest to the confusion over pastoral identity in congregations and in me. In *Pastoral Identity*, Webster offers a refreshing perspective, calling congregations to move beyond an obsolete Christendom model and into a 'household of faith' model of church leadership found in the New Testament. This book will challenge, encourage, and motivate you to think differently about the call to lead your congregation."

—Rev. Dr. Jeremy Vaccaro,
Senior Pastor, First Presbyterian Church, Fresno, CA

"Contrasting the 'counterculture household of faith' with the 'institutional Christendom church,' Webster takes his readers back to the future, calling pastors to embrace the calling of the New Testament church. He argues that the decline of Christian cultural influence is an opportunity to return to the difficult yet dynamic simplicity of pastors serving as shepherds rather than CEOs. This timely book will challenge pastors and parishioners alike to rethink their expectations for the church and give them practical guidance for tapping back into what makes it life-giving."

—Will Kynes, PhD,
Associate Professor of Biblical Studies, Samford University

"Pastoral ministry within Protestant and evangelical churches may not yet have reached the point of crisis, but it certainly seems wounded. Sadly, part of the wound is self-inflicted, as many pastors have been unwittingly trained in models of ministry incompatible with the New Testament. Webster's book offers a much-needed corrective: not a model based on control, implied hierarchical distance between pastors and parishioners, and pseudo-professionalism; but a model based upon mutuality, communal giftedness, friendship, and accountability. One may not agree with every point, but one should listen—and listen carefully—to Webster's words of pastoral wisdom. They are a balm for the wound."

—Phillip A. Hussey,
Pastor, Christ Fellowship Church, St. Louis, MO

# PASTORAL IDENTITY

## True Shepherds in the Household of Faith

## Douglas D. Webster

KREGEL MINISTRY

Printed in the United States of America

23  24  25  26  27 / 5  4  3  2  1

*Rick & Kathy Preibisius*

# CONTENTS

# PREFACE:
# THE UNLEARNING CURVE

The classical model of Christian ministry is rooted in medieval Christendom. The parish priest is the vicar of Christ and the singular representative of the church. The pastor exercises authority over all church ministries: preaching, celebrating the sacraments, officiating at weddings and funerals, administering Christian education, visiting sick parishioners, counseling, evangelizing, offering spiritual direction and more general care of souls, and running the church. The impact of this pastoral legacy separates clergy from laity, burns out pastors, and reduces the congregation to an audience of passive recipients of spiritual services.

Over the centuries traditions and habits shaped pastoral identity and overshadowed the way we carry out pastoral ministry today. This book explores the difference between a pastoral identity rooted in the early church's experience of the household of faith and a traditional pastoral identity formed in a nominally Christian culture. My aim is to understand and compare the relationship between pastors and people in two quite different settings: in the counterculture household of faith and in the institutional Christendom church. My premise is that pastoral ministry needs to undergo "a process of unlearning a way of working that destroys life."[1] Long-standing institutional habits distort pastoral identity, the impact of the gospel,

---

1    Eugene H. Peterson, *The Pastor: A Memoir* (New York: HarperOne, 2011), 4; see also 41.

and the meaning of following Jesus. I seek to revisit what it means to be a pastor among the people of God in a gospel-shaped household of faith rooted in the Bible, centered in Christ, and led by the Spirit.

I teach pastoral theology in an interdenominational seminary. The dialogue around the nature and practice of pastoral ministry is often lively. I don't have to convince my students that ministry is important. They are committed to Christ and his church, and they are eager to serve others in the name of Jesus. It is a rich experience to interact with believers from a variety of traditions, including Baptists, Anglicans, Methodists, Presbyterians, Lutherans, Pentecostals, and nondenominational churches. We have common ground in the Scriptures as we seek to develop the nature and purpose of pastoral ministry in congregations rooted in the fellowship of Jesus. Regardless of our tradition, there is plenty of room to be the kind of pastor envisioned by the Lord Jesus and the apostles.

CHAPTER 1

# SHARED WISDOM

*When I looked around me and observed churches in competition with one another for their share in the religious market, hiring pastors to provide religious goods and services for a culture of God consumers, I wanted nothing to do with it.*

—Eugene Peterson

To be involved in guiding a church in worship and mission is a great honor. It is a privilege to be called by a congregation to preach the whole counsel of God, to work alongside committed disciples, and to encourage the church's growth in Christ. There will always be frustrating personalities to contend with and plenty of unexpected challenges. We may confront a host of problems—including our own sins, emotional weaknesses, poor decisions, and physical limitations—but the beauty and power of gospel ministry outweighs these negatives. Whatever the burdens may be, they are overshadowed by the joy of the gospel.

I have enjoyed pastoral work so much so that I'd love to start all over again. What if it was possible to begin again, as if for the first time, with the biblical wisdom and Christian maturity acquired slowly, painstakingly over time? Life doesn't work that way, but I can dream. Instead, the tide comes in and the tide goes out, and a new generation of pastors comes in to give leadership and sacrificial service. Fantasies aside, our bodies and minds wear out. I tell my friends, I used to have more energy than time; now I have more time than energy. The spirit is *still* willing, but the flesh is weak.

When I was a young pastor and seminary teacher, I identified with the Lord's word to Jeremiah, "If you have raced with men on foot and they have worn you out, how can you compete with horses?" (Jer. 12:5) After eleven years in Canada, where our three children were born, and I earned a PhD from Toronto School of Theology, took a full-time seminary position, and pastored a small urban church, we decided to move back to the United States so that I could accept a position as the lead pastor of a church in Bloomington, Indiana.

The church in Toronto held a retreat to say goodbye to our family and to welcome the new pastor. I anticipated an enormous sense of relief, but instead I was overwhelmed by what lay ahead. I wanted a finish-line feeling. I wanted to hear, "Well done, good and faithful servant" (Matt. 25:23). But instead, I heard God say, "You have only just begun. Get going." The admonition to Jeremiah echoed in my soul, "If you stumble in safe country, how will you manage in the thickets by the Jordan?" (Jer. 12:5). Thirty-six years later I can identify with God's word to Daniel, "As for you, go your way till the end. You will rest, and then at the end of the days you will rise to receive your allotted inheritance" (Dan. 12:13). Many of us are somewhere in the middle between the admonition to "get going" and the commendation to "go your way; you can rest until the end." One of my colleagues reminds me that Daniel was pushing ninety when the Lord suggested retirement, adding, "Doug, you may still have years of work ahead of you."

## RELEARNING WHAT IT MEANS TO BE A PASTOR

This book wrestles with the difference between a pastoral identity rooted in Christendom and a pastoral identity rooted in the household of faith. By *pastoral identity* I mean how pastors see themselves, their roles, and their responsibilities, as well as how their congregation sees them. By *Christendom* I mean an enculturated version of Christianity based on religious tradition, church affiliation, and cognitive assent. By *household of faith* I mean the body of Christ, the ecclesial assembly of Christ's followers, whose belief, belonging, and behavior are radically transformed by the gospel of Jesus Christ. A Christendom church reflects the dominate values of the culture, and the countercultural household of faith reflects the values of Christ's kingdom.

My working premise is that a Christendom approach to pastoral leadership and congregational identity no longer fits our cultural situation and is a poor reflection of a biblical understanding of the church and its leadership. The New Testament reflects a dynamic synergy between congregational identity and pastoral identity. We seek a renewed understanding and practice of what it means to be a pastor in fellowship with the priesthood of all believers, serving in a Christ-centered community shaped by the gospel.

Pastoral identity in the household of faith transcends denominational traditions and is committed to mutual submission in Christ, every-member ministry, the gifts of the Holy Spirit, the priesthood of all believers, costly discipleship, and God's global gospel mission. Pastors are called and trained to preach the gospel, to equip the saints for works of service, and to work within the fellowship of believers in prayerful dependence upon the Lord. Pastors realize that their ordination vow is subordinate to their baptismal vow (their highest vow). Pastors embrace the humble authority of their responsibility.

Thankfully, we are headed back to the future, a future vividly described for us on the pages of the New Testament. The cultural compatibility and accommodation that have served the church for generations is no longer a viable option. The gospel cuts a swath through both religious and secular culture. Both sides reflect the reality of ideological captivity and cultural conformity. The followers of Jesus Christ have no other recourse than to see themselves as "chosen outsiders" living in a radically pluralistic culture. We are "resident aliens" living in our home culture. We are removed from the religious establishment, and we have little legitimacy in the secular world. We need to *unlearn* the habits of Christendom and embrace the *back to the future* New Testament understanding of the body of Christ.

We need a pastoral identity that fits the cultural realities described in 1 Peter, because that is our future and in many places the future has already arrived. The apostle Peter's letter is important because it develops the believer's foreign status in fresh ways that Christ's followers have not typically embraced. It critiques postbiblical Christianity in the West and inspires a no-fear discipleship in the global church. Peter's focus is not on how the bad the culture is, but on how good the Christian is called to be, even when confronted by social hostility.[1]

In the 1980s and 1990s, mainline Protestants and market-driven evangelicals accommodated to cultural forces in order to maintain cultural respectability and popularity. Christianity was secularized by pluralism on the one hand and pragmatism on the other. This was done to impress distinctive constituencies and to stave off an inevitable clash with culture. Evangelism in postbiblical Christendom came across as either spiritualized political correctness or Christianized self-help. Christianity across the spectrum attracted admirers to an iconic Jesus but failed to make disciples of the Lord Jesus.

Christianity's cultural captivity is real. Mainline Protestantism continues to offer a politicized ethic heavily influenced by secular culture, while market-driven Protestantism offers a psychologized gospel influenced by consumer-oriented, felt needs. Christendom, whether conservative or progressive, is steeped in religious tradition and privatized spiritual experience. It makes no difference whether the parish or congregation utilizes ancient liturgies or modern rock-

---

1    See Douglas D. Webster, *Outposts of Hope: First Peter's Christ for Culture Strategy* (Eugene, OR: Cascade, 2015), 1.

out praise music. Sometimes the line between Christendom Christians and countercultural Christians, between religious confidence and Christ-centered confidence, runs right through a congregation. The admirers of Jesus and the followers of Jesus sit side by side in the church pew. Christendom fosters passive recipients of spiritual services; the household of faith disciples gifted followers with a passion for Christ. Christendom stands for America-first Christianity; the household of faith stands for Christ and his kingdom.

America today is like first-century Rome, and the followers of Jesus Christ are challenged to embrace their "chosen exile" status. They are strangers in their home culture, missionaries in a familiar but foreign land. Now is not the time for Christians to bemoan the loss of religious clout and resent the power and influence of our secular age. The god of American civil religion is dead, and the Triune God—Father, Son, and Holy Spirit—is the only God who lives. There is no generic deity around which we can gather as a nation and pay our respects, but eventually every knee will bow, and every tongue confess that Jesus Christ is Lord.

## THE NEW TESTAMENT MODEL

The New Testament teaches that believers refuse to be defined primarily by their ethnicity and nationality; they belong to Christ and are subject to Christ's rule and reign. They are citizens of the kingdom of heaven both now and for eternity. This new identity inevitably leads to a clash with secular and religious cultures. Yet these chosen outsiders and resident aliens form a noncompetitive holy community. They have not been called by God to flee the world, nor have they been called to fight the world. Christ never intended his followers to withdraw into their own tight-knit culture—to become separatists, narrow-minded, and hard to get along with. First-century Christians did not impress the world as hostile and rigid and angry. Their form of offense—the offense of the cross—was and is the most winsome and attractive "offensiveness" that human culture has ever known. They understand and feel their own sinfulness and they experience the brokenness of the fallen human condition. But by God's grace they experience the power of God's sacrificial love and their responsibility to the ministry of reconciliation.

The New Testament church is committed to the sanctity of human life. The church's pro-life stance is for the unborn, the poor, the victims of injustice, the disabled, the addict, the refugee, the abused, and the exploited. The New Testament church upholds a biblical sexual ethic with conviction and compassion, practicing sexual purity outside of marriage and fidelity between a man and woman in marriage. The church is centered in Jesus Christ who alone offers personal and social salvation. Redemption and reconciliation are foundational to the life and ministry of the church. We are not in a position to impose our Christian convictions on the culture at large. We humbly and compassionately commend biblical truth and the Jesus way to a broken and hurting culture. The impact of Jesus's kingdom ethic and his call to make disciples of all nations replaces the American dream of the good life with a gospel life marked by the cross. Jesus challenges American exceptionalism and global superiority with the Great Commandment and the Great Commission. "The Holy Spirit forms church to be a colony of heaven in the country of death. . . . Church is a core element in the strategy of the Holy Spirit for providing human witness and physical presence to the Jesus-inaugurated kingdom of God in this world. It is not that kingdom complete, but it is that kingdom."[2]

The apostle Peter refused to focus on how bad the world was. Instead, he focused on how good the Christian should be. He asked,

> Who is going to harm you if you are eager to do good? But even if you should suffer for what is right, you are blessed. "Do not fear their threats; do not be frightened." But in your hearts revere Christ as Lord. Always be prepared to give an answer to everyone who asks you to give the reason for the hope that you have. But do this with gentleness and

---

2    Peterson, *The Pastor*, 110.

respect, keeping a clear conscience, so that those who speak
maliciously against your good behavior in Christ may be
ashamed of their slander. For it is better, if it is God's will,
to suffer for doing good than for doing evil. For Christ also
suffered once for sins, the righteous for the unrighteous,
to bring you to God. (1 Peter 3:13–18)

The unlearning curve is steep if we want Jesus and his truth to be
at the center of the way we work. This kind of learning is a whole
lot harder than learning Greek and Hebrew. It is easier to master
church history than to deal with our inherent self-centeredness
and the religious legacy of Christendom. We are shaped by internal
habits and cultural forces that we are hardly aware of. We often
have as much to unlearn about what it means to follow Christ as
we have to learn. The apostle Paul had both the unlearning and the
learning curves in mind when he wrote, "Do not conform to the
pattern of this world [the unlearning curve], but be transformed
by the renewing of your mind [the learning curve]" (Rom. 12:2).

When pastors focus on the things that really matter, they age
well, even when the maturing process is not without struggles and
setbacks. They're like fine wine. Immersed in worship, prayer, and
Bible study, year after year, for the sake of others, is a wonderful
vocational calling. I confess I don't know how to live life apart from
these rhythms of grace among the people of God. The exegesis of
the biblical text along with the exegesis of people becomes a vocational habit and spiritual discipline. I cannot imagine studying
the Bible apart from thinking about the people I encounter in and
outside of the household of faith. And I can't think about people
without thinking about God's Word. I am convinced that the Spirit
of Christ, who guides us in all truth, is at the center of the synergy
between the gospel text and people, believer and unbeliever alike.

Pastors who are mastered by the master don't think of themselves as experts or professionals. Their deep desire is to be faithful
and fruitful followers of Jesus Christ. Over time, their character is
shaped by the Spirit of Christ, their ethics reflect Jesus's kingdom

priorities, and their personality increasingly imitates Christ. Cultural blind spots remain, and nagging weaknesses persist, but they are moving in the right direction, even when it sometimes feels like for every step forward, they take two steps back.

I may not be able to start my pastoral ministry over again, but I would like to help others start better than I did. The purpose of seminary education is to prepare men and women for pastoral ministry in the household of faith. It is all about growing in the grace and knowledge of the Lord Jesus Christ. It is about learning how best to serve God's mission and the household of faith. It is not mainly about becoming knowledgeable with someone else's knowledge; it is about becoming wise with someone else's wisdom. Being an expert in the biblical text is not the same thing as loving and living the truth of God's Word. Debating the "ins and outs" of doctrinal disputes is not the same as becoming like Jesus and practicing the imitation of Christ. Scoring high on a Hebrew test is not the same as praying the Psalms, Jesus's prayer book, and letting the Psalms shape our understanding of sin and salvation. Church history deserves our study, but only if we bring our findings into the lived experience of the twenty-first-century church.

If I didn't believe that you could be wise with someone else's wisdom, I wouldn't be a pastor. Nor would I be a seminary professor or a parent, for that matter. Wisdom involves mutual give-and-take, always shared in the company of others. Know-it-alls are isolated and alone. Downloading information to make people more knowledgeable is not our true calling—entering into the wisdom of God is. The pursuit of knowledge for knowledge's sake or "knowing for the sake of being known as someone who knows" is not our goal.[3] Fear-of-the-Lord-wisdom is our shared calling and commitment. This is the true knowledge that Paul prays for on behalf of the church at Philippi: "that your love may abound more and more in knowledge and depth of insight, so that you may be able to discern what

---

3    James K. A. Smith, *On the Road with Saint Augustine* (Grand Rapids: Brazos, 2019), 144.

is best and may be pure and blameless for the day of Christ, filled with the fruit of righteousness that comes through Jesus Christ—to the glory and praise of God" (Phil. 1:9–11).

A pastor friend explained to me there are two kinds of books on being a pastor: those that work and those that are right. He lamented the difference between popular, practical how-to strategies for success in the world and counterintuitive strategies of sacrifice that only seem to work in the mind of God. But in the end, who are we trying to please and what do we really want?

If you think that the church is the single greatest force for good in the world with the oldest organization, largest participation, widest distribution, fastest growth, and highest motivation, then you will look to what works in the world—to the power, the image, and the credentials to make the church succeed in the world. But if you think the church is a persecuted body of resident aliens and chosen outsiders who are marked by the cross, then you will look for a pastoral identity in the household of faith that is marked by the cross and the hope of the resurrection.

Christendom works because of power: the power of numbers, budgets, buildings, and credentials. But the body of Christ lives to know Christ, "yes, to know the power of his resurrection and participation in his sufferings, becoming like him in his death, and so, somehow, attaining to the resurrection from the dead" (Phil. 3:10–11). The Christendom church is triumphalist. It is like the churches of Sardis and Laodicea (Rev. 3:1–6; 14–22). The household of God is humble. She is like the churches of Pergamum and Philadelphia (Rev. 2:12–17; 3:7–13).

Central Presbyterian Church in New York City was a dying Christendom church with a handful of die-hard members hanging onto their mainline liberal theology, cherished traditions, and enculturated religiosity. Scores of churches like this have faded away and their buildings have been sold off by the denomination. But in Central's case, several farsighted, committed believers envisioned reclaiming the church for the gospel. When the pastor who was rumored to have a drinking problem retired, they encouraged the

meager membership to call a gifted Bible preacher and a gifted worship leader. The members not only supported the move financially,
but they also gave unstintingly of their time and effort to expand
Central's outreach and to care for those who came. Solid gospel
preaching and Christ-centered worship created an "outpost of hope"
at 64th and Park. Believers from large vibrant churches in the area,
such as Redeemer Presbyterian Church, began to join the church
because they shared a vision for a vibrant household of faith with a
mission to the city. Students from Juilliard with a passion for Christ
participated on the worship team, and many gifted believers applied
themselves to a full range of ministries. Hospitality played a key
role in building up the body of Christ. After worshiping together
with the weekly Eucharist most of the congregation came together
for lunch in the fellowship hall—a really good buffet lunch. If you
came to Central for the first time and joined in on the fellowship
lunch, chances are you didn't leave a stranger. The key to reclaiming
the church for the gospel was not complicated. In fact, it was fairly
simple. It was Central's *Spirit-led devotion* to the apostles' teaching (the whole counsel of God) and to fellowship (genuine care
for one another), to the breaking of the bread (vital worship with
Holy Communion), and to prayer (true dependency upon God the
Father, Son, and Holy Spirit). Pastoral leadership was important,
but what made everything work so well were the many devoted lay
leaders. God used them to turn a Christendom church into a New
Testament household of faith.

# CHAPTER 2

# CHRISTENDOM AND THE HOUSEHOLD OF FAITH

*Pastoral ministry is the widest ranging, challenging vocation known to mortals.*

—Peter Leithart

*Human love constructs its own image of the other person. . . . It takes the life of the other person into its own hands. Spiritual love recognizes the true image of the other person which he [or she] received from Jesus Christ; the image that Jesus Christ himself embodied and would stamp upon all persons.*

—Dietrich Bonhoeffer

Traditional pastoral theologies emphasize the *special call* of the pastor. The hierarchical "shepherd and flock" model evolved in Christendom rendering the layperson a passive recipient of pastoral care. By the late third century the clergy embraced the Levitical priesthood as the prototype of their calling even though Jesus and the apostles rejected Judaism's priestly class, sacrificial system, and hierarchical leadership. The apostles never implied that the Levitical priesthood might be a model for pastoral ministry.

The Fourth Lateran Council emphasized a mysterious sacramental character of ordination making the celibate priest ontologically different from the ordinary Christian. William Willimon writes:

> Clergy were sacerdotalized and distanced from the laity. . . . Thus, many of our current notions of ordained ministry rest upon an innovation that occurred within the first two centuries of the church and which was brought to fulfillment in the first thousand years—*the creation of the laity*. . . . The laity are in effect, declared to be a people not set apart, a people who no longer share in Christ's high priesthood. Christ's priestly attributes are now read onto only one group of the baptized—the clergy—a sad development for the baptized.[1]

The classical tradition set the pastor apart as the singular representative of Christ in the church. The pastor alone was the one duly authorized to officiate the sacraments and exercise dominion over the functions of the church. The pastor was in charge of preaching, visitation, prayer, soul care, administration, and spiritual direction. The tradition perpetuated the idea among many Christians that unless the pastor visited and prayed over them, they had not been ministered to by the church. The legacy of the sacerdotal priesthood advanced the clergy/laity divide long after the Reformation removed the celebration of the Mass. Even though the pastor no longer offered a sacrifice to God according to the Levitical pattern, because Jesus Christ was sacrificed "once for all" (Heb. 10:10), the notion that the church needed a pastoral go-between prevailed.

The clergy were "specialized and stereotyped," combining civil and religious authority in a marriage of Christianity and culture. The act of the priest/pastor was to imitate the ministry of Christ in

---

1    William H. Willimon, *Pastor: The Theology and Practice of Ordained Ministry*, rev. ed. (Nashville: Abingdon, 2016), 42; see also 48.

prayer, teaching, spiritual direction, and leadership.[2] This legacy of medieval Christendom hangs over the modern professional pastor in ways not anticipated in the New Testament household of faith. All of this sets the clergy apart mentally and emotionally from the congregation in ways that are both unnecessary and unbiblical. If we are honest, this psychological and spiritual segregation is unwarranted and unhelpful.

Christendom's pastoral theologies assume the established hierarchy of the pastoral office, institutionalized religious authority, cultural accommodation, societal respect, a separation of responsibilities, and congregational passivity. A Christendom church is hardwired to be pastor-centered and spectator-oriented. Power flows from the top down. The real work of ministry is done by professional pastors who, like doctors, lawyers, and accountants, receive specialized training and credentialing in order to qualify them for carrying out their unique religious duties. This professional educational model reinforces the clergy/laity divide. Instead of seeing pastoral theology as a subset or a corollary of a theology of ministry, pastors are trained to think of themselves in a class apart from the rest of the congregation. The psychological and spiritual implications of a Christendom model have an impact on how pastors see themselves and the congregation.

Pastoral theologies generally begin with issues surrounding pastoral identity and the challenges facing pastors. Statistics on turnover and dropout rates of pastors are often cited. These traditional approaches assume a theology of church shaped by a Christendom model. Instead of affirming the disciple-making responsibility of the household of faith, the priesthood of all believers, the shared gifts of the Spirit, and every-member ministry, a Christendom approach affirms the controlling influence of the pastor and his or her responsibility for the ministry of the church. New Testament pastoral theologies represent an alternative model. They were formed in the

---

2    W. H. C. Frend, *The Rise of Christianity* (Philadelphia: Fortress, 1984), 405; see also 408.

household of faith and forged in persecution. They were organized around God's mission and promoted a theology of ministry built on every-member ministry, shared leadership, and pastoral authority. Traditional pastoral theologies are fundamentally different from the New Testament model of the church and ministry.

We expect pastors to be gifted by the Holy Spirit, skilled in interpreting and communicating the Word of God, and spiritually wise. Their gifts, devotion, and challenging work should be recognized and affirmed by the congregation. But with that said, too many pastors lean on a faulty religious tradition to bolster their position and their ego. It is hard to resist the professionalism and protocols of the Christendom model. They perpetuate the notion that their ordination entitles them and only them to function in certain specified ways. They act as if all of the preaching, presiding, and officiating belong to them by special right, and in the course of exercising their office they unwittingly belittle the gifts, training, leadership, and insights of their gifted congregation. This is not entirely the pastor's fault. Pastors and parishioners have colluded in promoting the pastor's need-meeting responsibilities and reducing the congregation to religious consumers.[3]

Swiss theologian Emil Brunner (1889–1966) argued that the church as we know it rests on a misunderstanding. By the third and fourth centuries sacramentalism and the episcopal office merged to produce the institutional church. The dynamic fellowship of the body of Christ described in the New Testament evolved into a hierarchical organization. The "supernatural Christian community" was embodied in visible and external form—God's revelation and God's salvation *in action*. Brunner wrote:

> The Body of Christ is nothing other than a fellowship of persons. It is "the fellowship of Jesus Christ" (1 Cor. 1:9) or "fellowship of the Holy Ghost" (2 Cor. 13:13; Phil.

---

3    See Douglas D. Webster, *Living in Tension: A Theology of Ministry* (Eugene, OR: Cascade, 2012), 1:25.

2:21), where fellowship or *koinonia* signifies a common participation, a togetherness, a community life. The faithful are bound to each other through their common sharing in Christ and in the Holy Ghost, but that which they have in common is precisely no "thing," no "it," but a "he," Christ and His Holy Spirit. It is just in this that resides the miraculous, the unique, the once-for-all nature of the Church: that as the Body of Christ it has nothing to do with an organization and has nothing of the character of the institutional about it. This is precisely what it has in mind when it describes itself as the Body of Christ.[4]

Although she has a long history as the covenant people of God, the New Testament church emerged with power at Pentecost in the outpouring of the Holy Spirit. This miracle made the fellowship of Jesus into a community of the Word and Spirit of Christ that precedes the individual believer. "Jesus Christ is the Truth and as such He founds a communion of God and man which puts an end to all isolation. Therefore, Christian truth can be apprehended only in the Christian fellowship."[5] Brunner emphasized that the *ecclesia* was never an "it," a "thing," or an "institution," but always the Israel of God, the seed of Abraham, the elect priestly race, the people of God's own possession, and a communion of persons. It was not intended to be a "legal administrative institution."[6]

The unlearning curve for Jewish Christians must have been steep, because much of what they had associated with religion was no longer in the New Testament picture of the household of faith. The apostles put it boldly, "Neither circumcision nor uncircumcision means anything; what counts is the new creation" (Gal. 6:15). "Don't you know that you yourselves are God's temple and that

---

4    Emil Brunner, *The Misunderstanding of the Church*, trans. Harold Knight (1952; repr., Cambridge: Lutterworth, 2002), 10–11.

5    Brunner, *The Misunderstanding of the Church*, 14.

6    Brunner, *The Misunderstanding of the Church*, 16.

God's Spirit dwells in your midst?" (1 Cor. 3:16). They stripped away the old religion, without replacing it with parallel religious rituals and experiences. In its place was the revelation of God in Christ. Paul said it bluntly, "Do not go beyond what is written" (1 Cor. 4:6). Instead of being united by rules, habits, rituals, and officials, Brunner insists that "the fellowship of Jesus Christ is the work and product of His word and spirit."[7] The apostles themselves were never the foundation for the fellowship of Jesus. It was the historically rooted revelation of God that was foundational to the *ecclesia*. It was the apostolic *witness*, not the apostolic *office*. This is why Paul said, "For I resolved to know nothing while I was with you except Jesus Christ and him crucified" (1 Cor. 2:2). There is no hint in the New Testament of "a permanently authoritarian hierarchal organization of the church."[8] The *ecclesia* of Jesus Christ is God's people. "In Christ the elect are no longer subject to the ceremonial, cultic, and civil laws of Israel and Judaism."[9] And "a distinction between priesthood and laity has forever ceased to be tenable."[10] There is a clear distinction between membership in the community of believers and membership in a nation and race. Brunner sums it up this way: "So then the fellowship of Jesus is the true people of the covenant, whose history doubtless begins with the old covenant, but which only attains full reality though the living presence of the Risen Lord. But because the fellowship is nothing else than this people of God dwelling in the Spirit, it is in no sense an institution, but the living body of the living head."[11]

## THE IDEAL PASTOR

Tradition emphasizes the pastor's "special call" to the ordained ministry. The pastor is singled out as the church's unique repre-

---

7   Brunner, *The Misunderstanding of the Church*, 25.
8   Brunner, *The Misunderstanding of the Church*, 28.
9   Brunner, *The Misunderstanding of the Church*, 20.
10  Brunner, *The Misunderstanding of the Church*, 21.
11  Brunner, *The Misunderstanding of the Church*, 24.

sentative. He stands as a lone male figure before God on behalf of the church and represents the church to the world. He is the point person for God. In some traditions he is a Moses-like figure, the man with the vision, or an apostolic figure, the man with power. It is not surprising that the phrase *the ministry* became synonymous with the role of the pastor. Instead of situating spiritual leaders in the midst of co-laborers and fellow sufferers for the gospel, the pastor became singled out as the only person with unique responsibilities and an official office. He's the man, literally and figuratively.[12] He preaches the Word, administers the sacraments, presides over the leadership of the church, and basically runs the church, and when he moves on or passes away his portrait hangs in a prominent place.

Peter Leithart's description of the pastor reinforces this perspective:

> The ideal pastor would have the rhetorical panache of a Churchill, the compassion of Mother Teresa, the tenacity and courage of a Navy Seal, the intellect of a lawyer, the patience of Job, the vision of Ezekiel, the creativity of an entrepreneur, the management skill of a CEO, and the magnetic energy of a rock star. He must be exemplary in his devotion to Jesus and the uprightness of his character, and he must be everywhere for everything. A doctor comes when you are ill or injured. You ask for a lawyer when you face legal challenges. You hire a consultant to revive or expand your business. You call on the nurse or the hospice worker to care for aging parents. We have specialists for every moment and stage of life. But the pastor is a generalist. He is there at the birth, the bedside, through the trial and the lawsuit, when a child is fighting for life and when a parent is slipping into the grave. The

---

12  See Douglas D. Webster, "Mutual Submission in Christ," in *The Practice of Ministry: Faithfulness to the End*, vol. 2, *Living in Tension: A Theology of Ministry* (Eugene, OR: Cascade, 2012), 128–59.

pastor is a generalist in all the forms and varieties of human misery. If the pastor is a specialist, he is a specialist in
death, in actual physical death and in all the lesser shocks
of death that flesh is heir to. He is present at all these
grave sides as a representative of the Good Shepherd.[13]

When I have seminarians read this pastoral profile, they gasp and
roll their eyes. They claim it fits better with the apostle Paul's cynical
description of the super-apostles in Corinth than with a description
of Paul's ministry. I agree with my seminarians: this hyperbolic
profile of pastoral leadership is foreign to the New Testament description of pastors. My students identify with the second half of
Leithart's quote when he begins to describe the pastor as a generalist
who shows up at the point of human need. Pastors who make it to
the ER to comfort anxious parents whose daughter was hit by a car
are not rock stars. They're brothers and sisters in Christ who care.

Leithart singles out the pastor as "the visible, tangible presence
of Christ and the church at every moment of crisis." He is the office-
holder who has the privilege and the responsibility of showing up
at births and deaths offering in some distinct way the presence of
Christ. This Christendom model isolates and privileges the pastor
and renders the church passive, training them to wait on the pastor—not only to offer support at significant events, such as births
and deaths, but even to pray and read Scripture. Ministry doesn't
happen until the pastor shows up wearing a collar and holding a
prayer book.

Pastoral theologies tied to Christendom inflate the role of the
pastor and reduce the meaningful work of the body of Christ.
Reductionistic pastoral theologies replace a lively, caring, gifted
household of faith with the pastor who is ordained to carry out
"the ministry." As *the* representative of Christ, the pastor serves

---

13   Peter Leithart, "The Pastor Theologian as Biblical Theologian," in *Becoming
a Pastor Theologian: New Possibilities for Church Leadership*, eds. Todd Wilson
and Gerald L. Hiestand (Downers Grove, IL: InterVarsity Press, 2016), 22.

in place of the body of believers—that's the real problem. Thomas Oden warns, "The pastor had best not do anything that the body itself could do. The pastor's primary task is to equip the body, not try to do everything for the laity. It is pride and an overweening need to control that causes the pastor to attempt to do the work of the entire congregation."[14] But it is difficult to heed Oden's warning if we follow his theology, since he insists on the singular significance of the pastor:

> There are five incomparable days in the believer's life. The day one is born, when life is given. The day one is baptized and enters anticipatively into the community of faith. The day one is confirmed, when one chooses to reaffirm one's baptism, and enter by choice deliberately into the community of faith and enjoy its holy communion. The day one may choose to enter into a lifelong covenant of fidelity in love. The day one dies, when life is received back into God's hands. What do those five days have in common? Who is invited to share them all? They are incomparable, pivotal moments in life. Besides the family, what persons or professionals are welcomed into the intimate circle of significant participants in all of those days? *Only the clergy.*[15]

The frame of reference for Oden's understanding of the role and responsibility of the pastor is a nominally "Christian culture" comprised of people who generally self-identify as Christians whether or not they profess to follow the Lord Jesus. The context is not an Acts 2:42 household of faith, but the institutional church that offers religious services and spiritual care for all types of people associated with the church in some way. Parishioners look to the church

---

14   Thomas C. Oden, *Pastoral Theology: Essentials of Ministry* (New York: Harper-Collins, 1983), 156.
15   Oden, *Pastoral Theology*, 85 (emphasis mine).

to perform rites of passage and help satisfy their spiritual needs. Nominal Christians are often just names on a church roll until they need a pastor to perform a wedding or officiate at a funeral.

If we follow the Christendom model, the notion of the ideal pastor dies hard. The clergy/laity divide has deep roots in ancient religious tradition, but it is missing in the New Testament's description of the early church. When a pastor is told that he is indispensable and that "sinners are forgiven, saints restored, lives enriched and hearts consoled—*all by your mouth and hands!*"[16] we are hearkening back to the Christendom church. The legacy of the sacerdotal priesthood lingers in our concept of the "vicar of Christ," the "parish priest," the "senior pastor," and in our concept of the entrepreneurial, visionary "church planter."

By the time John Chrysostom wrote his treatise *On the Priesthood* in the fourth century, the office of the pastor was inflated into something that it was never intended to be. Ordination was limited to males because it was thought males represented God best. In John's day, women were considered inferior physically, mentally, and morally. Thankfully, today we know better. There is no female inferiority on any grounds. We need women and men to represent God: "So God created mankind in his own image, in the image of God he created them; male and female he created them" (Gen. 1:27). In addition to being male, pastors had to be celibate, not so much because of the burden of family responsibilities, but because of sex. It was deemed inappropriate and unclean for the Mass to be conducted by a priest who had sex the night before. Sex was beneath the dignity of the office.

The ancients spiritualized the office and separated the clergy from the laity in ways that seem almost superstitious. The church's interpretation of the Mass meant that the priest played an essential role in the salvation of his congregation. John believed that "only by means of these holy hands, I mean the hands of the priest," who

---

16   Harold L. Scnkbcil, *The Care of Souls: Cultivating a Pastor's Heart* (Bellingham, WA: Lexham, 2019), 29.

lifts up the body and blood of Christ are people saved.[17] This put enormous pressure on the priest to be altogether righteous: "The priest, therefore, must be pure as if he were standing in heaven itself, in the midst of those powers."[18]

John Chrysostom believed that the office of the pastor hearkened back to the Levitical priesthood and the awe-inspiring glory of the Holy of Holies. The priesthood played an essential role in mediating salvation. John writes, "Anyone who considers how much it means to be able, in his humanity, still entangled in flesh and blood, to approach that blessed and immaculate Being, will see clearly how great is the honor which the grace of the Spirit has bestowed on priests. It is through them that this work is performed, and other work no less than this in its bearing upon our dignity and our salvation."[19] The burden of the priesthood was too much for John. Chrysostom complained that people were ready to pass judgment on the priest as if he wasn't human, as if he was an angel, free from every type of infirmity. John did not challenge the priestly pedestal—he expected it. "Everyone wants to judge the priest, not as one clothed in flesh, not as one possessing a human nature, but as an angel, exempt from the frailty of others."[20]

By the time of the Reformation, the celebration of the Lord's Supper had undergone a complete transformation. It had gone from "a service of praise and thanksgiving, celebrated every Sunday by the whole community of faith" to a "clericalized" ritual performed by the pastor. When the priest lifted up the bread and wine from the altar and said, in Latin, "*hoc est corpus meum*," he claimed to be holding in his hands the very body of Christ and typically ate the host on behalf of the congregation.[21] The Reformation decisively

---

17   John Chrysostom, *On the Priesthood: Six Books on the Priesthood*, trans. Graham Neville (Crestwood, NY: St. Vladimir's Seminary Press, 1996), 73.

18   Chrysostom, *On the Priesthood*, 70.

19   Chrysostom, *On the Priesthood*, 71.

20   Chrysostom, *On the Priesthood*, 86.

21   Timothy George notes, "Our English expression, *hocus-pocus*, which we use as a kind of byword for something magical or incredible, comes from the

rejected the medieval Mass as a spectator event performed by a sacerdotal priest. The Reformers recovered the meaning of the cross. They confessed only one sacerdotal priest, the Lord Jesus Christ. However, the legacy of the inflated role of the pastor persisted.

## MESSIANIC EXPECTATIONS

There is a connection between the medieval sacerdotal priesthood and the messianic expectations Jesus encountered. Virtually everyone in Jesus's day was looking for a political messiah who would come and take over. The people, the religious leaders, and the Roman oppressors all envisioned a militant messiah who would wage war. When the messiah came, he would kick Rome out, establish his rule, and restore the glory of the Davidic kingdom. As anyone who has read the New Testament knows, Jesus was not that kind of messiah. A tradition based on misinterpretation and false expectations generated an understanding of the messiah that contradicted salvation history.

Jesus had to work to renegotiate the meaning of the Messiah as the crucified Savior in the minds and hearts of his followers every day of his ministry. This clash of messianic expectations dogged Jesus right up to his ascension. His disciples wanted to know, "Lord, are you at this time going to restore the kingdom to Israel?" (Acts 1:6). The Holy Spirit guided the early church into God's mission: the global impact of the gospel, the formation of the one new race in Christ, and the redemption of the world. But renegotiating the traditional messianic expectations involved a painful process.

Some time ago, I attended an installation service for one my students. He became the new senior pastor in a large, wealthy congregation. My friend is a humble and mature believer. He is a wise pastor, a gifted preacher, and a thoughtful leader. He is grounded in the Word of God and committed to the priesthood of all believ-

---

Latin words of institution, *Hoc est corpus meum.*" *Theology of the Reformers*, rev. ed. (Nashville: B&H Academic, 2013), 151.

ers. But if his installation service was any indication, he will have an uphill battle with a congregation that appears to be hoping more for a charismatic power figure in their proud church than a Christ-centered, humble pastor in the household of faith. No one questioned when a participating pastor applied Isaiah's messianic prophecy to their new pastor, "For to us . . . a son is given, and the government will rest on his shoulders" (Isa. 9:6). A passage that Christians believe applies specifically to the Incarnate One was co-opted in the moment to say something big about their new pastor. It was greeted with loud cheers and thunderous applause! I left amazed at the pressure this new pastor was under to meet his congregation's messianic expectations.

Most congregations are less open about their "messianic" pastoral expectations, but just as determined. Their search for a new pastor is carried out with a set of spiritual qualifications. They are looking for a good preacher with spiritual wisdom who can help lead the church in worship and mission. But what they usually don't say, yet want, is a business-savvy CEO with personal charisma who knows how to run a religious organization. They want someone popular enough to attract the crowds and sharp enough to run the staff, raise the budget, and administer the whole operation. This describes not only the pastoral position at the top but just about every other position on staff. Everyone is looking for "rainmakers," people who will make *it* happen. Leadership is expected to recruit an enneagram-profiled "dream team." It is reasonable to want the church to run well and for practical concerns to factor in to being faithful and fruitful. But do we know what it means for the church to run well? Are our expectations shaped by God's Word or by the business models of the world? It seems unreasonable to expect one person to do all this.

Pastors are tempted to live as if everything depended upon them. One night I had a dream from which I awoke in a cold sweat with my heart pumping. I had dreamed that our church was performing Handel's *Messiah* in a Sunday evening service. The whole church was excited and looking forward to the evening. The musicians had rehearsed for weeks, and the conductor was ready. On the day of the performance the congregation turned out, along with hundreds of visitors. It was standing room only and the anticipation of the gathered crowd was great. The energy in the room was palpable. There was only one problem: none of the musicians showed up. There was no orchestra, no choir, no soloists, and no conductor. It was my job to welcome everybody and open in prayer, but there was nothing to introduce. I was all alone. However, in my dream the congregation expected me to carry on as usual and perform the *Messiah*. You can imagine my relief when I woke up from the nightmare!

## A FALSE LITERAL

In addition to the Christendom tradition of messianic expectations, we face the problem of the *false literal*. The early church adapted to the absence of a literal, physical Jesus. The risen and ascended Lord was in their midst in the real presence of the body of Christ, the church. Jesus was present to the fellowship of believers not in a mediating pastor figure, whether by ordained office or charismatic personality, but in the reality of the Spirit of Christ indwelling the church. The danger of a "false literal" confronts the church today whenever a "sacred" substitute is found for the risen Christ. It is tempting to put someone or something in the literal place of Jesus. It may be a pastor, it may be church music, it may be the worship ritual. It is whatever manipulates and motivates believers to live out their faith vicariously through a "Christian idol."[22]

The temptation to create a substitute for Jesus is real and may be subtle. The physical immediacy of a person with status or charisma or intellect or devotion is a symbolic proxy for the believer's one-on-one relationship with Christ. It is tempting to live vicariously through the spiritual life of the pastor. His faith becomes my faith, his spirituality

---

22   See Douglas D. Webster, *The God Who Kneels: A Forty-Day Meditation on John 13* (Eugene, OR: Cascade, 2015), 119–21.

counts for my spirituality. It makes sense for pastors to pray not only for us but on our behalf. They pray so we don't have to pray. Pastors study the Bible for us, because we're too busy. We have other things to do. Besides, pastors know more than we do. They can pray the Psalms, extend pastoral care, and meet with the poor in our place and on our behalf. For, after all, God has set them apart for these sacred duties and we pay them to do pastoral work. Of course, the obvious danger, which doesn't seem all that worrisome, is that we become passive recipients of secondhand spirituality.

Jesus was constantly renegotiating the true meaning of the Messiah, just as pastors are constantly having to reclaim the New Testament meaning of pastoral care. In order to be faithful and fruitful, pastors unlearn the expectations and terms of endearment fostered by the traditions and legacy of Christendom. While household-of-faith pastors seek to overcome the clergy/laity divide, Christendom pastors encourage it. Traditional messianic expectations coupled with the temptation of the false literal accentuates the terms of endearment. People expect their pastors to exemplify their cultural version of Christianity. It is difficult for pastors to negotiate the boundary between meaningful contextualization and compromising cultural accommodation. Churches in the Christendom tradition tend to want their pastors to represent their societal values, embody their hopes and dreams, and reflect their cultural identity. If they can't have Jesus in the flesh, they want someone they can look up to. They want a Christ figure who is always there for them.

## APOSTLES VS. SUPER-APOSTLES

Whenever the apostles addressed the issue of leadership explicitly, they did so in the context of putting the health and holiness of the body of Christ first. They prioritized the household of faith and the priesthood of all believers.[23] Spiritual direction

---

23  Tom Greggs, *Dogmatic Ecclesiology: The Priestly Catholicity of the Church* (Grand Rapids: Baker Academic, 2019), 101. Greggs writes, "Despite the

on leadership in the New Testament always comes after the big picture of discipleship is addressed practically. The meaning of life together sets the stage for the apostles' teaching on the plurality of pastoral leadership. The apostle Paul's highly relational conclusion to his letter to the church in Rome commends men and women for their hard work. These church leaders are variously described as deacons, coworkers, fellow prisoners, dear friends, apostles, and brothers and sisters in Christ. They are a blessing to many people because of their faithfulness. They have risked their lives for the sake of the gospel (Rom. 16:1–16).

Paul pushed back against the church's worldly leadership expectations. He took issue with the so-called "super-apostles" whose way of speaking, exercising power, and competing for attention collided with Paul's vision of true apostolic leadership. The biblical profile of pastoral leadership countered the Corinthian profile of powerful and prestigious leaders. It is likely that Christendom's expectations have more in common with Corinth's super-apostles than with the apostle Paul's vision of pastoral leadership. And the transition from a culturally compatible super-apostle to a servant of Christ can be a rough one.

George made it his mission to challenge my theology of the household of faith and pastoral leadership. His Christendom model longed for the glory days when the church was the religious home to city officials, prestigious weddings, and state-sponsored funerals, when the pastor was a member of Rotary and the country club and the campaign chairman for the United Way. Back in the day the ushers wore white gloves and tails. Our San Diego sanctuary was modeled after an East Coast cathedral and the pride of the music program was a 101-rank organ, with more than five thousand pipes, one of the best on the West Coast. George wanted me, *his pastor*, to

---

preoccupation of much literature on the topic of priesthood relating to specific officeholders in the church, the only mention of a priesthood other than Christ's is in relation to the whole community." See also 1 Peter 2:9; Rev. 1:5–6; 5:10; 20:6.

be "out there" hobnobbing with the urban elite, greeting the Navy ships when they came to port, creating events that would draw crowds and the attention of the media.

George failed to negotiate a back-to-the-future transition from 1950s Christendom to the New Testament household of faith. Calling Christians "resident aliens" or "chosen exiles" made no sense to him at all. As far as he was concerned, he was attending a downtown mainline church with an impressive past and, hopefully, a successful future. He didn't realize that the culture had shifted right under his feet. He refused to acknowledge that today's believer faces a countercultural existence. George was a religious insider, not an elect exile. For those with ears to hear and eyes to see the New Testament describes the social impact of the gospel and its inevitable clash with culture. I wasn't sure that it registered with George that 1 Peter was in the Bible and that it gives the church an accurate description of the situation facing twenty-first-century believers.

What was happening at 3rd and Date in downtown San Diego was not going over very well with George. Even so, our church was steadily growing. Our membership was solid, just under nine hundred, and our weekly attendance was around eight hundred. The average age of our members was growing younger. The lost were coming to Christ, small groups were thriving, and outreach ministries were going strong. We baptized infants and adults with parental and personal confessions of faith in Christ. Times were set aside during the week for prayer in the sanctuary. But George was not satisfied with our "slow growth." He wanted exponential growth. So, he mounted a campaign to undermine my leadership. He called and visited pastors throughout the state, culling together data and anecdotes to be used against me. Everything good that was happening elsewhere was an indictment against my leadership because it wasn't happening in our church. In the process of his campaign, George turned a couple of previously supportive elders against me. Eventually these manipulated elders left the church, but not before souring others on my preaching and my leadership. George was toxic. Congregational meetings became George's platform for strengthening his campaign.

He seldom spoke up himself, choosing instead to use surrogates to represent his position. George came to church every Sunday. He hung out in the fellowship hall but stopped coming into worship, or if he did he left before the sermon.

The prayerful and vocal leadership and support of many of the elders and members of the congregation was reassuring. George's adult daughter, visiting from out of state, greeted me after a worship service. Through tears she explained how sorry she was for what her father was doing to the church and to me. She will never know how much that meant to me. A few elders spent literally hours trying to dissuade George from his negative campaign. They reported everything good that was happening, but it wasn't good enough for George.

Several pastors, serving churches hundreds of miles away, called me after a personal encounter with George. Their calls began with a similar refrain, "Do you know what this guy George is saying about you?" George's criticism was so bold and blatant, and the encouragement from friends so helpful, that it seemed okay to let the whole matter play out. I don't mean to sound overly spiritual, but not reacting and trusting the Lord to work it out seemed like the only way to go.

Then one day, I received a call from Joanie, George's wife. She asked if I would I come to the hospital right away. George was in the ICU. He suffered a massive stroke and collapsed at his computer. I rushed there, held his hand, and prayed for him and his family. George never regained consciousness and the church held his memorial service several days later. Joanie, who was always faithful in worship, became a deacon the next year and served the church beautifully. George's ideal pastor may have been like one of the super-apostles in Corinth, an impressive individual by worldly standards, a person who commanded a following, performed with excellence, and exuded charisma. I don't think he envisioned an *unimpressive* apostle Paul as his pastoral model.

Paul gave believers an obvious choice between two radically different ways of being the church. He contrasted the way of the cross with the spirit of the age. He warned the Corinthians "not [to] go beyond what is written," insisting on servant leadership marked by the cross. Paul insisted we are "fools for Christ," a people who have experienced all manner of privation and persecution for the sake of the gospel (1 Cor. 4:1–13). Paul's emphasis was on the responsibility of "brothers and sisters" to humbly exercise their gifts for the unity, worship, and mission of the body of Christ. He never singled out the "senior pastor," nor did he lay out unique responsibilities for the office of the pastor. Nevertheless, he was clear on how he wanted people to see himself and his coworkers. They were servants of Christ and stewards of the mysteries of God (1 Cor. 4:1).

Paul used the word "mystery" (μυστήριον) to refer to the revelation of God, previously hidden but now made known. Paul contended that the true meaning of wisdom and maturity was not found in human speculation or self-discovery, but in God's revelation. There were no hidden mysteries belonging to a spiritual elite, only the "open secret" that the Spirit of God had revealed for all to believe—the crucified Lord of glory.

We should want all spiritual leaders to see themselves in this way: slaves of Christ and stewards of the mysteries of God. The work of a pastor is not running around catering to people's felt needs. We are not blessing the admirers of Jesus; we are building up the followers of Jesus. We are not satisfying religious consumers. We are equipping the saints for the work of ministry. All believers are called to salvation, service, sacrifice, and simplicity. You and I may be called to different responsibilities in the household of faith and in the mission of the church, but we are all called!

## MENTAL MODELS

Charles Duhigg, in his *Smarter, Faster, Better,* compares two in-flight plane emergencies.[24] One flight ended in disaster, the other landed safely. There were two radically different outcomes due to

---

24  Charles Duhigg, *Smarter, Faster, Better: The Secrets of Being Productive in Life and Business* (New York: Random House, 2016), 71–102.

vastly different pilot reactions. Air France Flight 447 was bound for Paris from Rio de Janeiro with 228 people on board. One of the pilots of the Airbus A330 became disoriented when ice crystals froze the airspeed indicators and automatically turned off the auto-flight system. If he had done nothing the plane would have continued flying safely, but he pulled back on the command stick, causing the plane's nose to nudge upward and the aircraft to gain altitude.

As the plane continued to ascend into the increasingly thinner atmosphere, the craft's lift began to deteriorate. A loud chime went off in the cockpit as well as a recorded voice warning: "Stall! Stall! Stall!" But instead of lowering the plane's nose the pilot continued to pull back on the stick, pushing the plane's nose further into the sky. With warning alarms sounding, both pilot and copilot became disoriented, trying to find the answer to what to do with the streams of data generated by the flight computers.

Psychologists call this *cognitive tunnel thinking*. Instead of taking a step back to assess the overall picture, the pilot fixated on emergency procedures used to abort a landing. He maximized the plane's thrust and raised the nose of the plane. At thirty-eight thousand feet, the air was so thin that it only increased the severity of the stall. Cognitive tunneling led to reactive thinking, dooming Flight 447 and killing all on board.

One year later, Qantas Airways Flight 32, flying from Singapore to Sydney, sustained massive damages when an oil fire led to an explosion that ripped apart an engine turbine, shattered the engine, punctured the left wing, and severed electrical wires, fuel hoses, a fuel tank, and hydraulic pumps. The plane's computers gave step-by-step instructions for dealing with each problem, but as system after system failed and issues escalated there was no way to keep up with the cascading data.

The experience and training of the pilot kicked in. He shouted to his cockpit crew, "We need to stop focusing on what's wrong and start paying attention to what's still working."[25] As a copilot began

---

25   Duhigg, *Smarter, Faster, Better*, 98.

ticking off what was still operational, the pilot imagined that he was flying the first plane he ever flew, a little Cessna. In the surrounding chaos he took control of his mental model and flew the plane. Instead of being inundated with information and overreacting to the stream of unprioritized data, he pushed panic and confusion aside and flew the plane. Qantas Airways Flight 32 landed safely because the pilot never stopped flying the plane. He never yielded to data and the cockpit chaos. He focused on a mental model that allowed him to fly the plane.

Charles Duhigg writes, "To become genuinely productive, we must take control of our attention; we must build mental models that put us firmly in charge."[26] There are many things about church and culture today that threaten to overwhelm pastors as they pilot the church. Distractions and contingencies abound. Internal and external pressures can shock and confuse, lulling us to fixate on our problems, resulting in cognitive tunneling. We are tempted to lose track of what it means to belong to a pastoral team in the household of faith. Instead of following Jesus deeper into his word and prayer we turn to the myriad of clever voices for solutions and distractions. We need to stay focused on what it means to belong to Christ's church, the household of faith.

## PAUL'S MENTAL MODEL FOR MINISTRY

Tim Gombis suggests that many sincere, well-meaning Christians operate with Paul's pre-conversion power-through-strength mode of ministry. "In his pre-Christian ministry mode, Paul was seeking to bring about God's purposes through coercive power, verbal and physical violence, and by transforming sinners into Torah-observant Jews in an effort to move God to save Israel."[27] Before Paul met the risen Jesus, his mental model of ministry was

---

26  Duhigg, *Smarter, Faster, Better*, 102.
27  Timothy G. Gombis, *Power in Weakness: Paul's Transformed Vision for Ministry* (Grand Rapids: Eerdmans, 2021), 33.

shaped by his *image* as a Pharisee of the Pharisees, the *credentials* that made him a "Hebrew of Hebrews," and his *merit*-based righteousness according to the law (Phil. 3:4–6). Before his encounter with the risen Lord Jesus on the road to Damascus, Paul's mental model of ministry was Joshua's conquest strategy of Canaan. The violence of Israel's invasion of Canaan in the days of Joshua was replicated in Paul's zealous persecution of Christians. Paul believed he had a *biblical* reason for attacking and killing Christians. He judged them to be a blasphemous cult claiming to follow a false messiah, whose death on a cross proved that he was an impostor from the beginning. Paul's status-conscious, merit-based, ethnic tribalism justified coercive power in the name of God.

Gombis parallels Paul's unconverted religious zeal with today's Christendom pastors who focus on accruing power, promoting their position, measuring success by numerical growth, and projecting an aggressive "them against us" cultural confrontation. As a Pharisee, Paul was trained to see ministry as a militant nationalist. But when he met the risen Jesus on the Damascus road everything changed. The reality and hope of the resurrection were something that could not be understood from a human perspective. It was counterintuitive. God became fully human and humbled himself "to the point of death, even death on a cross" (Phil. 2:8). The crucified and risen Messiah invites us into the fellowship of his suffering and the power of his resurrection, into a life and a future that replaces Joshua's conquest strategy with Jesus's great commandment or great commission strategy.

Paul, Gombis concludes, "came to see that his ministry mode of power and coercion was tragically misguided, as was his personal pursuit of staking a claim for resurrection based on prestigious credentials and an approved social status. The realities of God's resurrection program dramatically upended his expectations."[28] Now, instead of being a Pharisee of the Pharisees he was a sinner saved by grace. Instead of impressing people with his religious credentials,

---

28   Gombis, *Power in Weakness*, 50.

he embraced the weakness of the cross. Instead of communicating with eloquence and superior wisdom, he resolved to know nothing except Jesus Christ and him crucified. Instead of the power of the world, he took God at his word, "My grace is sufficient for you, for my power is made perfect in weakness" (2 Cor. 12:9). Gombis sums this up beautifully when he writes,

> The counterintuitive way that God triumphed in Christ— by Jesus humbling himself and going to the lowest place, dying a shameful death on a Roman cross as a common criminal—determined Paul's mode of ministry. He embraced weakness and shame in his ministry, a radical departure from his former pursuit of prestige, exalted social status, and engagement in competition with fellow ministers. Paul had discovered the logic: since God raised Jesus from the dead and exalted him based on his faithful obedience unto a shameful death, God would flood Paul's life and ministry with resurrection power the more he lived and ministered from weakness and embraced the social shame that inevitably came his way.[29]

---

29  Gombis, *Power in Weakness*, 56.

# EXCURSUS: ILLUSTRATING THE DIFFERENCE

|  | Christendom Church | Household of Faith |
|---|---|---|
| **Church and Culture Identity** | Parishioners tend to profile their church by their pastor, denomination, and location. Religion is an important sphere of societal influence alongside education, business, politics, sports, and community service. The senior pastor is their religious representative in the community. The church building is a source of pride and denominational church membership provides a distinctive and easily understood identity. | Members identify with their church relationally rather than institutionally. They shy away from denominational labels and see themselves as followers of Christ. They have come to see themselves as countercultural resident aliens and the church as a called-out community of believers. They are not looking for societal recognition as they seek to be "salt and light" in their social and occupational setting. |
| **Pastoral Authority / Leadership** | The pastor is in charge of church ministry and determines the programs and persona of the church. The office of the pastor is vested with considerable authority regardless of the denominational affiliation and polity. There is a hierarchical leadership structure built on various committees, departments, and programs. The board of deacons or the session of elders or the vestry of lay leaders signs off on initiatives of the ordained, professional staff. | There is a plurality of pastoral leadership that is integrated in the life of the church that is made up of godly and gifted men and women who serve with a high degree of consensus, mutual submission, and personal responsibility. The line between paid and unpaid church leaders is blurred and pastoral oversight is conveyed through a team approach to ministry. Administrative efficiency is sometimes sacrificed for the sake of shared leadership and meaningful partnership in ministry. |

# EXCURSUS: ILLUSTRATING THE DIFFERENCE

|  | **Christendom Church** | **Household of Faith** |
|---|---|---|
| **Worship, Baptism, and Holy Communion** | The nature and style of worship are governed by the liturgical tradition of the denomination, whether Baptist, Pentecostal, or Episcopalian. Deviations from the set pattern are uncommon and usually unwelcome. The musical genre remains constant and in mainline churches is performed by paid, professional musicians. Baptism is a rite of passage couched in denominational expectation and religious custom. Holy Communion tends to be celebrated formally and is scripted according to the denominational tradition. | Gospel-centered worship in Word and Sacrament focuses the life and passion of the church. Under the care of gifted worship pastors, a wide variety of musical genres and avenues of expression are used to praise the Lord. Worship reflects the diversity of the body of Christ. Only Christ-confessing believers receive baptism, whether infant baptism or believer's baptism by immersion. Weekly Eucharist is increasingly a customary practice and is accompanied by a simple liturgy after God's Word is preached. |

# EXCURSUS: ILLUSTRATING THE DIFFERENCE

|  | Christendom Church | Household of Faith |
|---|---|---|
| **Mission and Evangelism** | Mission endeavors require programming, budgets, volunteers, and support from the pastor and other leaders. Mission constitutes a range of activities, from outreach to the homeless, to tutoring immigrants, to musical performances that enrich the community, to sponsoring overseas mission trips. Evangelism also requires programs, strategies, budgets, volunteers, and support from the top. Support for missions and evangelism tends to run in cycles of concern and effort arising from advocates who want the church more involved in helping the world and sharing the gospel. | Mission is what the church is all about. Jesus's Great Commission and Great Commandment constitute the marching orders of the church militant and missional. Everything about the church, from worship to outreach, from children to seniors, from local concerns to global outreach is about proclaiming and living out the gospel. The household of faith intentionally and prayerfully becomes a company of disciples serving, locally and globally, Christ and his kingdom. This requires programming and planning for specific endeavors to love the world for Christ's sake. |
| **Preaching and Teaching** | Sermons often convey the genre of their denominational tradition and echo the sentiments of their religious culture. Seldom do sermons vary from the prescribed range of topics and concerns popular in their setting. Sermons tend to be more therapeutic than theological and are usually addressed to the individual. | Sermons preach the whole counsel of God and proclaim the impact of the gospel in every aspect of life. Preaching is part of an integrated whole-church, whole-Bible curriculum that supports the intentional teaching ministry of the church. |

# EXCURSUS: ILLUSTRATING THE DIFFERENCE

| | Christendom Church | Household of Faith |
|---|---|---|
| | They convey an uplifting and inspiring message with humor, anecdotes, and human-interest stories. They identify with the human plight and offer hope. Christian education is geared to popular topics that will generate interest. | Becoming like Christ is the essential concern of expository preaching, Sunday classes, and small group ministries. During special times of the year, such as Advent and Lent, preaching and small groups share an integrated biblical focus. |
| **Relational Life, Family, and Youth** | Institutional concern for children, families, youth, singles, couples, and seniors is organized around staffing, programing, and facilities, which are designed to meet the needs of each age group and life stage. The senior pastor, program directors, and board leadership arc happy when all parties are satisfied with the organizational and relational administration of these various programs. The emphasis of these specialized ministries is intended to enhance the positive experience of church. This is especially true of children and youth ministries. | The cross-generational, cross-cultural fellowship of Jesus centers the household of faith in a shared worship experience with a family-based children and youth ministry. Relationships are oriented more theologically than therapeutically out of a desire to grow in the grace and knowledge of the Lord Jesus Christ. The shared concern of the body of Christ is to establish mature disciples at every life stage and develop genuine friendships that go beyond a person's peer group. Spiritual leadership is a collaborative endeavor between people, parents, grandparents, and pastors. |

# EXCURSUS: ILLUSTRATING THE DIFFERENCE

|  | Christendom Church | Household of Faith |
|---|---|---|
| **Small Groups, Friendship, and Accountability** | Efforts are made to enhance the friendliness of the church. Ushers are trained, digital pictorial directories are made available, experts in assimilation and communications are hired, along with a small-groups coordinator. Men's and women's groups are organized and volunteers are celebrated. In addition to a printed newsletter mailed to residences, a high-quality website keeps everyone up to date on the latest news. The purpose is to keep people coming back—if not every week, at least once a month. | Meaningful spiritual and relational growth is built into the DNA of the household of faith. People are known by name and prayed for regularly. If a parishioner misses a Sunday, those in attendance notice. There is opportunity, every Sunday morning in worship, in Sunday classes, in each other's homes, and in small groups, to go beyond friendliness to friendship. Genuine accountability has an opportunity to take root in the household of faith where you are known in the fellowship of Jesus. |

# CHAPTER 3

# THE HEROIC PASTOR

*Few pastors will deny that on Sunday mornings we look across the pulpit into the pews with a sense of envy. Everyone else in the church came because they wanted to be there. They're all free. They don't have to praise God even when they feel like cursing today. They could have spent the morning with the New York Times and a good cup of Starbucks without anyone thinking that their call was in jeopardy.*
—Craig Barnes

A pastor looks out over the congregation before the sermon. As the choir sings, the pastor prays that the sermon he is about to deliver will meet the spiritual needs of a diverse congregation. The pastor sees a young couple just back from their honeymoon. They're all smiles, looking as if life couldn't be better. At the other end of the row is an eighty-year-old widow who recently buried her husband. For forty years she sat in that pew with him and now she sits alone. Behind her is a family of four appearing a bit hassled and tense. Their restless teenage son, with his brightly colored orange hair, makes it obvious that he doesn't want to be there. Nearby sits a well-dressed CEO with his fashionable second wife. As he prays and the choir sings, the pastor feels the burden of ministering to a full range of human need, knowing that the sermon he preaches may be the only opportunity in the course of the week for God's Word to minister to these people's lives.

Most of the congregation drives to church. They park their cars, exchange a few words and smiles with the assigned greeters, and enter the sanctuary. They receive a bulletin from a friendly usher and sit down to wait for the service to begin. They see religion as personal, a private affair of the heart—something between them and God. The preacher addresses their existential longings. After the sermon, the benediction signals a speedy departure. There is no lollygagging in the parking lot. It is time to get home. The rest of the day is spent in leisure, watching sports, shopping, and getting ready for the week ahead.

Christendom has been practicing "social distancing" for years. Relational connectedness and rootedness are not usually part of the DNA of a Christendom church. A percentage of baptisms (christenings) and weddings are performed as institutionalized public service. The clergy officiate infant baptisms for second-generation families whose only appearance at church is on Christmas and Easter. Weddings are conducted for couples who have little regard for Christ and the church, but they like the aesthetics of the sanctuary for a wedding.

By way of contrast, the household of faith is a true fellowship of believers. It is "true" as opposed to "ideal." There is a shared sense of the human condition, of every-member responsibility and of mutual care. The pastoral team and mature leaders are essential for the work of the church. They are responsible for nurturing a sense of connectedness and rootedness. It is part of the DNA of the church. In the situation described above, relational care belongs to the whole church, not just the pastor. The newly married young couple rush over to the widow to see how she is doing. They assure her of their prayers, even as she shows interest in their recent honeymoon. For her part, the gray-haired older woman looks the orange-haired teenager in the eye. She smiles and asks how school is going. She knows that being older can sometimes be an advantage in relating to young people. She aims to show him she cares. The CEO's quick exit is intentional, but kindly interrupted by one of the church elders who invites him and his wife over for dinner next week. This is a quick glimpse into the household of faith at work. The religion of Christendom is a private affair, but the worship of the household of faith is a shared commitment.

My wife and I spent several years commuting between Birmingham and New York City on weekends to help a fledgling congregation in Manhattan emerge from the ashes of theological liberalism. The leadership team behind this renewal movement needed a credentialed pastor and a biblical preacher. I fit that description. At first I was skeptical that we could pull it off, but I underestimated the commitment of the body of Christ at 64th and Park Avenue. We began that journey with uncertainty and queasy stomachs, but it became a wonderful experience. Frankly, the laypeople in that congregation had a stronger devotion and vision for gospel renewal than we did. They invested considerable time, money, and passion into seeing a dying church come alive in Christ.

Harry Emerson Fosdick's old church became the launching pad for a gospel-centered, Christ-honoring household of faith. While Howard Edington preceded me with strong evangelical preaching and Jason Harris followed me with great preaching and leadership, it was mature disciples who led the transformation. I don't want to downplay the rough times, the sleepless nights evoked by criticisms and power plays, but through it all God's blessings prevailed. We were helped by a host of servant leaders: gifted musicians who knew how to lead worship, devoted lawyers and businesspeople who gave countless hours to administration, capable servants who hosted fellowship after worship services, and spiritually minded elders and deacons who gave pastoral care. I had never before served a church where a person in the hospital was visited not only by me, the pastor, but by multiple elders and deacons as well. Relational issues, financial needs, and counseling concerns were addressed by lay leaders. Pastoral care and witness became the responsibility of the household of faith. We were all mindful of the need to pray for the church.

Thomas Oden's traditional conception of ordination confers on the pastor an office that rises above the disciple's baptismal vows in importance and significance:

> There remains a line as thin as a hair, but as hard as a diamond, between ordained ministry and the faithful layperson. For in ordination spiritual gifts are recognized and the gifted are commissioned to preach and celebrate the sacraments and to act in the name of the whole church and with the authority of the apostolic tradition. Through ordination a sacramental office is conferred on the ordained that is not so conferred on all baptized Christians. It is not merely through the personality of the minister, but by reason of the office, that *the pastor becomes an effective symbol of the grace of God acting through the church.*[1]

Pastoral authority is vested in the office rather than in gifted proclamation of the word, biblical discernment, godly character, and the gifts of the Spirit. Rightly understood, all of these qualities are necessary for ordination and essential for pastoral ministry, but when one person is vested with the office of pastor, the qualifications are subsumed under a title. By virtue of the office, the pastor becomes the singular authority figure of the institutional church. He is the presiding officer and chief decision maker in the Christendom church. The *vicar of Christ* is Christ's representative, the personal embodiment of our heavenly Father. The pastor becomes a *symbol*, standing for Christ *above and apart*, rather than a fellow disciple *in and of* the household of faith.

In *The Art of Pastoring,* David Hansen writes that "being a symbol of God is an exceedingly weak pastoral role" because "symbols reinforce what people already believe."[2] Pastors who

1   Oden, *Pastoral Theology*, 88.
2   David Hansen, *The Art of Pastoring: Ministry without All the Answers* (Down-

become symbols stand before the people like the American flag or the Queen of England. They simply mirror back to the people their hopes and dreams. Instead of being a catalyst for meaningful discipleship, they meet and placate people's expectations. Hansen encourages pastors to become parables pointing to Christ, rather than symbols representing people's preconceived ideas. Jesus used parables to come at the truth indirectly, provocatively, even subversively. Symbols reflect our thinking about religion; parables cause us to reflect on our discipleship and renew our commitment to Christ.[3]

## RETHINKING THE HEROIC PASTOR

If Jesus intended a top-down, hierarchical model of pastoral leadership, the New Testament's description of leadership would have been remarkably different. Attention would have focused on organizational structure, credentialing, succession plans, training, and qualifications. Instead, we have a character profile of a person who is a member of a pastoral team, a spiritual leader who is respected in the household of faith and in the larger society as a fully devoted follower of the Lord Jesus (1 Tim. 3:1–13).

There are several factors that challenge the notion of the heroic pastor, which I will state briefly here, then drill down deeper into:

1. The biblical description of the Christian life is meant for all believers.
2. Pastoral theology is a subset of an overarching theology of ministry.
3. The seminary's curriculum is primarily a disciple-making curriculum.
4. There is only one biblical standard for holiness; there is no double standard.

---

ers Grove, IL: InterVarsity Press, 1994), 131.
3    Webster, *Living in Tension*, 1:79.

1. All believers, pastors included, receive the same biblical instruction on living the Christian life. By the grace of God, we are all called to wholehearted discipleship. The New Testament letters offer a concise and comprehensive description of what it means to be a Christian in the household of faith. Explicit passages on pastoral leadership are rare and often come at the end of a detailed and thorough description of the ordinary Christian life.

It is an interesting exercise, in this respect, to compare explicit passages on parenting with the explicit passages on pastoring in the New Testament. Everyone agrees parenting and pastoring are two very important concerns in the household of faith. But biblical passages that specifically address these responsibilities are few and far between.[4] In other words, what is good for discipleship in general is also good for leadership in the church and home.

2. The only pastoral theology known in the New Testament is a pastoral theology rooted in the household of faith. Everything the apostles said to pastors, elders, and spiritual leaders was said in the context of the whole household of faith. Pastoral theology was and remains fully integrated in and subsumed under a theology of discipleship and a kingdom ethic. What is involved in being a pastor is always considered as a subset of what it means to be an obedient follower of the Lord Jesus. "What's true in the ministry of Christ's called and ordained servants is also true in the life of discipleship of every baptized Christian."[5] The New Testament emphasizes the call of God, the universal priesthood of all believers, costly discipleship, and God's mission for the global church. When the apostles describe their responsibilities as "servants of Christ" and "stewards of the mysteries of God" they do so in the context of the body of Christ and the shared mission of the church.

---

4     Greggs, *Dogmatic Ecclesiology*, 54.
5     Senkbeil, *The Care of Souls*, 121.

3. The seminary curriculum, which is designed to train pastors, is essentially a disciple-making curriculum. Seminaries offer an in-depth understanding of God's Word, a thorough grasp of salvation history, and a keen awareness of the doctrinal development of the Christian faith. There is little taught in seminary that does not belong in the church as essential training for disciples. Courses in spiritual formation, preaching, counseling, worship planning, and global missions are appropriate for all Christians, and all of these courses ought to parallel what is taught in the church.

Pastoral theology is the culmination of theology and ethics, spiritual formation and counseling, preaching and missions. Pastoral theology is all about thinking Christianly about a range of issues: one's calling, self-understanding, leadership, suffering, worship, mission, preaching, witness, and resilience. It is not about thinking secularly about professional etiquette, public relations, staff searches, the IRS, and salary negotiations. Pastors need spiritual direction on conducting weddings and memorial services and insight into these important worship times are embedded in biblical theology, not institutional "best practices."

There are only a few specialized courses that may be reserved for the seminary graduate student. Language courses in Greek and Hebrew may be a step too far for most students of the Bible, but all Christians ought to have a sense of how language works and the challenge of translating ancient languages into modern languages. An in-depth understanding of philosophical theology and contemporary theological debates may be a steep hill to climb for most believers, but necessary intellectual terrain for pastors to cover. Pastors are not religious experts with insider information on the secrets of the soul. Nor are they tasked with proving to the world that they play a meaningful role in society. They are ordinary believers who have the spiritual discernment, intellectual drive, and emotional desire to pursue theological training and the spiritual disciplines for the sake of the household of faith.

It should be emphasized that all Christians need to grow in the grace and knowledge of our Lord and Savior Jesus Christ. We are all called to discern what is best and to be filled with the fruit of righteousness. We all need to embrace the fact that all truth is God's truth. We all need a theology of faith and vocation, and a relational grasp of a theology of the church. Seminary education was meant to serve the church as a whole, and the best courses are those that can be carried over from the seminary into the pulpit, Sunday classes, and small group Bible studies.

4. There is no *biblical* double standard between pastors and laity, even though there is a long-standing tradition of just such a double standard. Ambrose, an early church theologian, distinguished between *ordinary precepts* which all Christians ought to obey, and the *counsels of perfection* followed by priests and monks. R. E. O. White explains,

> The "commandments" were gospel precepts binding upon all who would be Christians at all; the "counsels" were binding upon all who sought the higher life of Christian "perfection." So developed the distinction of "religious" and "lay" Christians; of expert, "professional" obedience from that of ordinary Christians whose second-class discipleship must be content to fulfill, in family life and the work of the world, the simple basic precepts of the Gospels; while those favored with a "vocation" to perfection can alone hope to attain the evangelical counsels of the higher life.[6]

Everything the Bible says to pastors, it says first to disciples. Ordination sermons challenge pastors with Jesus's command, "Feed my lambs" (John 21:15), or they inspire with Paul's example, "In your relationships with one another, have the same mindset as Christ Jesus" (Phil. 2:5). They embolden pastors with Joshua's courage,

---

6    R. E. O. White, *Christian Ethics: The Historical Development* (Atlanta: John Knox, 1981), 50.

"Be strong and courageous" (Josh. 1:9), or with Jeremiah's passion, "His word is in my heart like a fire, a fire shut up in my bones" (Jer. 20:9). But when these same texts are preached on Sunday morning, they call ordinary believers to a costly discipleship. Ironically, we set pastors apart in ordination services to become what every believer is expected to become—a faithful follower of Jesus Christ. Setting pastors apart to fulfill responsibilities that they are uniquely gifted and trained to fulfill need not set ordinary believers up for excuses and false dependencies.

The Bible affirms a spirituality that grows and matures in the midst of ordinary life. Our relationship with God was meant to mature in the midst of pressures and problems, relationships and ambitions. The ancient understanding of the "counsels of perfection" virtually removed the majority of Christians from the serious contemplation and pursuit of maturity. The word of God stresses, however, that the purpose of "admonishing and teaching everyone with all wisdom" is that "we may present everyone fully mature in Christ" (Col. 1:28).

## ADMIRERS VS. FOLLOWERS

The household of faith needs to become familiar with the gifts of the Spirit, the priesthood of all believers, mutual submission in Christ, and every-member ministry. The emphasis in pastoral theology and a theology of ministry is on discipleship. The goal is for all believers to grow in the grace and knowledge of the Lord Jesus Christ. British theologian and missiologist Lesslie Newbigin describes the interrelation between pastoral theology and the church this way:

> I hope I have made clear my belief that it is the whole
> Church which is called to be—in Christ—a royal priest-
> hood, that every member of the body is called to the
> exercise of this priesthood, and that this priesthood is to
> be exercised in the daily life and work of Christians in the

secular business of the world. But this will not happen unless there is a ministerial priesthood which serves, nourishes, sustains, and guides this priestly work. The priestly people need a ministering priesthood to sustain and nourish it. Men and women are not ordained to this ministerial priesthood in order to take priesthood away from the people, but in order to nourish and sustain the priesthood of the people. Just as we observe one day of the week as "the Lord's Day," not in order that the other six days may be left to the devil but in order that they may all belong to the Lord; so we set apart a man or woman to a ministerial priesthood not in order to take away the priesthood of the whole body but to enable it.[7]

In Christ, we are all meant to be disciples gifted by the Spirit, set apart for holy vocations, and equipped for good works. Congregations prayerfully appoint a pastoral team from within the body of Christ that evidences the teaching gifts, men and women who preach the Word of God faithfully and effectively, and who have the necessary discernment to lead the household of faith. The responsibility of pastoral leadership serves to enhance every-member ministry. It does not diminish it. The fruit of pastoral theology is the organic growth of uncomplicated, ordinary believers—followers of Jesus Christ, who are God-dependent, shaped by the Spirit, strong in character, obedient to the Word of God, engaged in ministry, and faithful to the end.

Our family was on vacation and on Sunday morning we walked to the little green church not far from the beach. The amiable pastor was dressed in a Hawaiian shirt and shorts and his sermon text was from Philippians. He began his sermon by wondering whether he and the apostle Paul would get along. Would they be good friends? "Don't get me wrong," he said. "I have a lot of respect for Paul. He

---

7    Leslie Newbigin, *The Gospel in a Pluralistic Society* (Grand Rapids: Eerdmans, 1989), 35.

was after all an apostle and he penned the book of Romans, but if you ask me, he was a very uptight guy. I don't think there was a lot of fun in his life, and I like fun! You know the apostle Paul was just too serious for me."

The congregation, largely made up of vacationers like us, loved the pastor's sermon angle. Amused, they nodded their approval, and chuckled to themselves. If they had to choose, they'd probably go with the guy in the Hawaiian shirt rather than a serious-minded, scarred-up apostle. It was a clever pastoral ploy, part of his shtick: win over the casual, lighthearted folks. Get them on your side. Create a religious environment that does not clash with the rest of their lives. A sermon should leave people feeling better about themselves than when they came. What you don't want to do is anything that intimidates or makes things too serious. We are seriously unserious. My sons were young at the time, but they shot a glance toward me as if to say, "This guy can't be serious." I didn't expect the sermon to get much better, and it didn't, but the tourists loved it.

Søren Kierkegaard called the church that no longer distinguishes between admirers and followers "Christianity without Christ." The Danish Christian thinker warned his generation in the 1850s of a Christ-less Christianity. He believed that the life of Jesus "from beginning to end, was calculated only to procure *followers*, and calculated to make *admirers* impossible." He writes, "His life was *the Truth*, which constitutes precisely the relationship in which admiration is untruth."[8] As admirers are confronted by the truth, Kierkegaard reasons, a moment comes when the demands of the truth bring an end to their admiration: "But when *the truth*, true to itself in being the truth, little by little, more and more definitely, unfolds itself as the truth, the moment comes when no admirer can

---

8    Sorén Kierkegaard, *Training in Christianity and the Edifying Discourse Which "Accompanied" It*, trans. Walter Lowrie, eds. John F. Thornton and Susan B. Varenne (Princeton, NJ: Princeton University Press, 1957), 232. Emphasis mine.

hold out with it, a moment when it shakes admirers from it as the storm shakes the worm-eaten fruit from the tree."[9]

Pastors are called to proclaim the gospel in Jesus-like ways, with pastoral care and prophetic impact. Moral and spiritual discipline accompany friendship and love. They admonish their fellow disciples and teach the truths of the faith. Like the apostle Paul, they "try to please everyone in every way," but they are quick to add, as Paul did, that their purpose is not for their own good but for the good of many, "so that they may be saved" (1 Cor. 10:33). And lest there is any confusion, Paul adds, "Follow my example, as I follow the example of Christ" (1 Cor. 11:1). Paul insisted on doing everything for the sake of the gospel as defined by the grace of Christ and the example of Jesus. This is why Paul said to the believers in Galatia, "If I were still trying to please people, I would not be a servant of Christ" (Gal. 1:10). *Unlearning* Christendom's people-pleasing burden frees pastors up to make disciples. Pastors are not in the business of meeting consumer demand and providing religious services.

## PASTORS AS FARMERS

Farming impresses me as a helpful analogy for pastors (2 Tim. 2:6). Both endeavors are labor-intensive, and working the soil is akin to working the soul. Farmers, especially those working traditional family farms, respect the balance of forces in the ecosystem. Pastors, likewise, must respect God's sovereign will and timing. Farmers participate in a delicate and patient dance with nature. Pastors live in the ebb and flow of the Spirit's leading and power. The highly programmed institutional church that services religious consumers is akin to a monocultural industrial farm. The church, though, needs to aim for the complexity of mature discipleship rather than the efficiency of a popular product.

*The Biggest Little Farm* is a beautifully scripted, photographed film that follows the experiences of a young couple for seven years as they

---

9    Kierkegaard, *Training in Christianity*, 239.

seek to form a sustainable farm—a farm in harmony with nature.[10] John and Molly Chester moved from their two-bedroom apartment in Santa Monica, California to an old abandoned avocado orchard on a two-hundred-acre, arid stretch of land one hour north of L.A. Everyone thought they were crazy, but they dreamed of growing food—a wide variety of food, organically—and raising animals—all sorts of animals, humanely. All the monocultural farms around them were industrial-scale, cash-crop ventures, but John and Molly were purpose-driven by a conviction that the health of our food is determined by how it is farmed.

John and Molly wanted to farm in harmony with nature. They wanted to farm without chemical fertilizers and pesticides. Their first challenge was dead, lifeless soil, devoid of microbial life. They had to rip out tons of brush and weeds and bring the soil back to life through irrigation, compost fertilizer, and cover crops. It was a long, slow process to infuse the soil with microorganisms, but they wanted to get it right. Their mentor, Alan York, quipped, "There's never enough time to do it right; always enough time to do it over." Their objective was to emulate the natural ecosystem by aiming for as much biodiversity as they could plant and grow. This meant planting a wide variety of fruit trees, cover crops, and vegetables, along with raising chickens, sheep, cows, ducks, pigs, bees, and livestock guarding dogs. As Molly said, "Every animal you'd see in a children's book." Before they were done, they were growing two hundred different things. Eventually, Alan explained, diversity leads to simplicity and harmony—a sustainable farm develops a self-perpetuating, self-regulating ecosystem.

Biodiversity farming is analogous to growing a gospel-centered household of faith. If we cultivate the rich diversity of the priesthood of all believers, the wide variety of the Spirit gifts, and the social complexity of races, and if we build harmony out of the differences between women and men, young and old, educated and uneducated, rich and poor, we are on our way to experiencing the spiritual eco-

---

10   *The Biggest Little Farm*, dir. by John Chester, featuring John Chester and Molly Chester (New York: Neon, 2018), http://www.biggestlittlefarmmovie.com.

logical reality of the kingdom of God in Christ. John Chester said it
well, "A simple way of farming is just not easy." Likewise, pastoring
the simple way is not easy because it is dynamic and alive. Doing
life and ministry the Jesus way is simple, but it isn't easy.

I was surprised by how much drama was in this ninety-minute
documentary. The idealism of the traditional farm runs smack
dab into the destructive forces of nature. "Every step we take
to improve our land," Molly lamented, "just seems to create a
perfect habitat for the next pest." Their lush fruit trees attracted
gophers that ate the roots, and the beetles, snails, and swarms of
starlings ate the fruit. One year they lost 70 percent of their fruit
crop. But "observation followed by creativity" meant facilitating
and depending on natural predators, like coyotes and snakes, to
keep the gopher population in check. It meant building nests for
owls to drive the starlings away and letting the ducks loose in the
orchards to feast on snails. As the herds of cows and sheep grew, so
did the mounds of manure that attracted swarms of maggot-pro-
ducing flies. Solution: let the chickens roam everywhere and eat
the maggots. Coyotes evaded electric fences and devastated their
chicken population multiple times, until they found a guard dog
brave enough to fend off the coyotes and disciplined enough not
to eat the chickens.

Neither running a traditional farm nor growing a household
of faith is smooth sailing. It seems that for every two steps forward, farmer and pastor alike take at least one step back. When
John and Molly were starting out, Alan York promised that by the
seventh year farming would feel like surfing. And, sure enough, in
their seventh year they felt like they had tapped into the power of
nature. The soil was rich, and the aquifers were full. The interplay
between crops and animals was flourishing, and the wildlife were
returning to what was now a livable habitat. For John and Molly,
the rhythm of farming had reached a sweet spot—a dynamic equi-
librium, a kind of rest. It was still a lot of hard work, but Apricot
Lane Farms had been transformed. Their "biggest little farm"
was productive, profitable, and beautiful. They were convinced

that the old way of farming—*in harmony with nature*—was the future of farming. I like the analogy between farming in harmony with nature and pastoring *in harmony with the New Testament*. Growing the household of faith organically means embracing the power of the gospel to make one new creation out of our complex spiritual, social, and cultural diversity. We need a biblical vision for a sustainable household of faith—a vision for "the biggest little church."

# EXCURSUS

## ORGANIC/RELATIONAL CHURCH GROWTH INITIATIVES FOR THE HOUSEHOLD OF FAITH

1. Focus on the basics: teaching the Word; building relationships, engaging in worship, and learning to pray. Prioritize multigenerational worship and cross-cultural mission. In an effort to take God more seriously than budgets and buildings, build the leadership team on the foundation of prayer and Bible study.

2. Discover how God-centered worship is the most effective tool in evangelism, fellowship, disciple-making, and mission. Make worship the chief goal of God's mission in your congregation. Learn to pray the Psalms and cultivate a comprehension vision of life that proclaims Jesus is Lord. Use the Psalms to focus meditation, to guide the call to worship, and to give depth to corporate worship. Bring all those involved in directing the worship services together for monthly prayer and planning sessions.

3. Emphasize the importance of resting on the Sabbath for the rhythm and pattern of family and personal life. Reclaim Sunday from sports and shopping for the sake of spiritual growth, fellowship, and worship. This can be done positively through teaching and personal examples, rather than dogmatically and legalistically. Do not fill Sunday with church business meetings.

4. Nurture a congregation of worshipers by weaning people from a spectator mentality and a performance expectation. Move away from entertaining, crowd-pleasing performances. Look at worship as an integrated whole, rather than only at its component parts. Diminish the "master of ceremonies" role in favor of a liturgy that focuses on God through great hymns, songs of praise, prayer, preaching, and Holy Communion. Begin worship with a call to worship; include prayers of confession and intercession. Identify the Lord, and not the religious consumer, as the audience of your worship.

5. Restore the true purpose of preaching by guiding people in the whole counsel of God. Overcome the unwarranted distinction between preaching and teaching and edification and evangelism. Preaching should be biblical teaching that moves, comforts, instructs, and challenges the body of believers. Authentic preaching will also be effective in answering the questions and concerns of earnest seekers. Solid preaching that edifies and inspires believers is the best form of evangelism. Feeding a congregation a constant diet of entry-level evangelism neither builds up believers nor wins true converts.

6. Permit seekers and strangers alike easy access to information about the church. Invite key people who are gifted in building relationships to help befriend newcomers. Create a non-pressured approach to new people that will avoid both forced friendliness and uncaring anonymity. Personally invite visitors to a home fellowship group or a special gathering where they can meet the leadership team. Show people love, but do not chase them or cling to them.

7. Integrate the proclamation of the Word of God on Sunday morning with small-group ministries and youth programs. Not only is good preaching shaped by the Word of God from beginning to end, but it also shapes the biblical community. The

Bible ought to shape the leadership and administrative culture of the church. Real preaching enlivens the whole church to God's mission in the world.

8. Start early in training children to hear and interact with the Word of God. Move away from amusing young people and socializing adults. Encourage young people and adults to prepare for Sunday school and small group fellowships by working through a Bible-study lesson. This will increase thoughtful participation and deepen the church's appreciation for the Word of God. Mentor parents to become their children's primary spiritual directors. Pastoral care begins in the home.

9. Use the sacraments of the church, baptism and Holy Communion, in a theologically thoughtful way. Whether a particular church adheres to believer's baptism by immersion or covenantal infant baptism, the church has the opportunity and the responsibility of affirming the meaning and integrity of personal commitment to Christ. The sacraments should be preserved from a perfunctory administration. Leaders should meet with individuals and families who desire baptism and use this as an occasion to strengthen their faith in Christ.

10. Educate people in a disciple-making process that begins early and extends through life. Show practical interest in how the Christian life is worked out in the home and at work. Special studies for Christians in business, retail sales, law, science, medicine, education, law enforcement, and the arts will help people to think Christianly about their vocations.

11. Prepare high-school students to understand their culture from a Christian worldview. Using the Word of God, interact with the events, philosophies, music, personalities of the culture. Students should have at least a basic understanding of God and humanity, good and evil, pain and suffering, salvation, and

death. Carefully work through one of the Gospel accounts to develop a clear understanding of the life and purpose of Jesus.

12. Encourage mission trips. Begin close to home. These may include inner-city soup kitchens, nursing homes, hospitals, and day-care centers. Before students and adults go on African and Asian mission trips, they ought to become involved in local ministries. There are many opportunities to minister in the name of Christ without going far from home.

13. Network with believers from other cultures and with missionaries. Develop a direct relationship with a church or churches in another culture. This may mean a close relationship with an inner-city church, where members of a suburban church teach tutorials and help meet physical needs, while members of the urban church teach Sunday school classes at the suburban church. Build genuine friendships across cultural and ethnic boundaries for the sake of the kingdom. This will change the way we pray and use the Lord's money.

14. Pray to the Holy Spirit for an openness and sensitivity to the dynamic of God's work in your church. Ask the Lord to lead you to people in need: single parents, widows, international students, young parents with disabled children, foster parents, and the unemployed. Those who have not heard the gospel are everywhere, but it is often at the point of obvious need where people are most receptive to the gospel of Christ.

15. Expect the household of faith to evangelize through its countercultural distinctiveness rather than through cultural accommodation. Remember, it is God's called-out, visible community, set apart to be salt and light in a dark world. Quietly refuse to accommodate by catering to the world's expectations. When the church gathers, it is to glorify and praise God. Weddings and funerals are not social services to the community; they

are God-centered worship services. If they cannot be done in integrity, they should not be done.

16. Reverse the trend that makes the pastor a manager rather than a theologian, an administrator rather than a spiritual director, an emcee rather than a worship leader. Under the auspices of the leadership team, delegate administrative responsibilities to gifted, capable people. Develop a team ministry approach that relies on the spiritual gifts and commitments of mature believers. Encourage the priesthood of all believers while maintaining the authority of the pastoral team.

17. Offer training for prospective leaders based on the biblical rationale, description, and expectation of leadership in the household of faith. Develop a mentoring relationship between mature, gifted leaders and those who show potential for leadership. In all areas of church life, appoint leaders who are holy in character and spiritually wise. Constituency representation should not be a primary qualification for leadership in the household of faith.

18. Encourage membership in the body of Christ through a nurturing fellowship rather than an informational program. Inclusion in the church is on the basis of a clear confession of faith in Christ and baptism. Membership classes stress personal commitment and responsibility to the church and its mission. Spiritual direction emphasizes the priesthood of all believers, every-member ministry, and the immense value of ministry outside the four walls of the church in the secular arena.

19. Practice preventative and corrective church discipline. Encourage nonthreatening conversations with church members about their walk with God, their growth in Christ, and their ministry responsibilities. Confront, rather than overlook, sinful behavior. Do this in a manner and spirit true to the counsel of the Word of God. Express a genuine concern for individual believers and

the integrity of the household of faith in order that Christians will not be left to struggle in their sin and the witness of Christ will not be damaged.

20. Remember that the life of the church and the growth of the body are under God's sovereign care. It is our responsibility to actively participate in the divine patience—waiting, watching, and working in the tradition and example of our Lord Jesus Christ. We make it our goal to do everything the Jesus way.[11]

These suggestions are offered as a practical New Testament guide to church growth, to encourage believers to apply themselves in ways that are faithful and fruitful. There is nothing trendy and innovative about this agenda. Implementation requires spiritual discipline rather than financial resources. It is a team effort, best executed by mature women and men in Christ, rather than by a charismatic leader. Genuine church growth cannot be bought or programmed. It is organic growth arising from the vital life of Christ in the household of faith.

---

11   See also Webster, *Living in Tension*, 2:171–75.

CHAPTER 4

# PASTOR AS FRIEND

*Nurturing friendship, I contend, is the first step pastors can take in nurturing a culture. Pastors are called to nurture a Christoform culture, one where the life, teachings, death, and resurrection, and ascension of Jesus are formative, and friendship is quite often the front door into that culture.*

—Scot McKnight

God designed us in such a way that the measure of our communion with God is reflected in the depth of our relationships with others. As Christians, we look at friendship from the unique perspective of God's love for us and Christ's love in us. The wholeness we find in Christ empowers us to make friends. These friendships consist in mutual respect, shared concern, and common cause. They involve a meeting of minds, an enjoyment of each other's company, and the freedom to feel at home with one another. Friendship with God and faithfulness to one another, then, are two sides of the God-centered sacramental reality we call life.[1]

Institutional Christendom frustrates and inhibits the formation of this kind of friendship within the fellowship of believers

---

1   See Douglas D. Webster, *Soulcraft: How God Shapes Us through Relationships* (Downers Grove, IL: InterVarsity Press, 1999), 71.

because it institutionalizes relational life through specialized job descriptions and successful programs designed to meet the needs of passive recipients. The demands of the organization crowd out the friendships born in organic relational life. There are gifted and dedicated Christians serving in a Christendom setting who do everything in their power to build fellowship, make disciples, and foster meaningful spiritual growth, but their efforts are sadly frustrated by impersonal, consumer-orientated structures. Multiple service times built around music and generational preferences tend define an audience, not a congregation. Jonathan Leeman makes the New Testament case for a gospel-grounded, single-service church structure that "demonstrates, proves, embodies, illustrates, incarnates, makes concrete, makes palpable and touchable and hearable and seeable the unity we possess in the gospel."[2] The gospel "produces its own kind of space" that glorifies God and knits believers together in holy fellowship.[3] "The gathered, assembled, congregated church is the kingdom of heaven made visible on planet earth. It's Christians bound together—experiencing the first fruits, the first taste, the first experience of God's society-creating rule."[4]

The organizational dynamics of the household of faith are meant to nurture and enhance the relational life of the congregation. Organization and order are necessary, but they are there to serve the organic character of communion with God and community with one another. Christians who are gifted relationally and who embrace their call to strengthen the fellowship of believers will find working in the household of faith freeing and fulfilling. The pressure to preserve the institution will be replaced by the freedom to grow the church spiritually, organically, and numerically. Instead of following a business plan for a corporate culture, the household of faith follows a biblical balance of organic and

---

2    Jonathan Leeman, *One Assembly: Rethinking the Multisite and Multiservice Church Models* (Wheaton, IL: Crossway, 2020), 23.
3    Leeman, *One Assembly*, 57.
4    Leeman, *One Assembly*, 47.

ordered relational life centered in Christ for the sake of God's glory and human flourishing.

Associate pastors, whose senior pastors evaluate their performance by institutional metrics, struggle to harmonize what they learned in seminary with the demands of the job. There is a conflict of conscience when success is measured statistically, by increasing numbers and innovative programs, instead of by discipleship and prayer for spiritual growth. Christendom's vision of pastoral ministry proposes an alternative relationship with parishioners, a relationship that was never envisioned in the New Testament. Since the pastor is Christ's representative in a way that is distinct and different from his brothers and sisters in Christ, he is advised by his fellow pastors to find friends outside of his church family to prevent confusing his pastoral responsibilities with his ordinary friendships. Since he needs to be pastored by pastors, because he himself is a pastor, he is counseled to look for friends in "the company and support of colleagues in office." The pastor should find friendship among his "indispensable brothers," who know that "this office is bigger than any one of [them]."[5] This conception of pastoral friendship is reinforced by the legacy of the sacerdotal priesthood and the Christendom model of church and culture, as well as by the image of the CEO or of the politician who is always running for office. Even when it comes to friendship, then, the burden of ministry falls heavily on the pastor.

## A ONE-WAY STREET

Before leaving the pastorate to become a seminary president, Craig Barnes wrote an article for *The Christian Century* titled "Pastor, not Friend."[6] Barnes insisted that it is important for pastors to "maintain healthy friendships outside of the church," but in the

---

5   Senkbeil, *The Care of Souls*, xviii.
6   M. Craig Barnes, "Pastor, not Friend," *The Christian Century*, December, 27, 2012, https://www.christiancentury.org/article/2012-12/pastor-not-friend.

church pastors must "maintain a distinction between relationships of mutuality and those of service as a pastor." Barnes wrote that when the elders of the congregation ordained him to be their pastor, they were "being led by the Holy Spirit to push me away from them. They were essentially saying, 'We are setting you apart to serve us. So, you can't be just one of the gang anymore. Now you have to love us enough to no longer expect mutuality.'" Barnes continues: "It wasn't long after I stood up from the ordination prayer that I discovered this. But the elders have a hard time understanding the holy distance they created by their decision to make me their pastor." This is the high cost of ordination, says Barnes, "this lonely status of being surrounded by everyone in the church while always being the odd person in the room."

Ordination places the pastor on a one-way street of meeting needs. All the giving, caring, and responsibility flows in one direction from the pastor to the people. Barnes paints a bleak but realistic picture of the Christendom pastor who is drowning in obligation and unrelenting pressure. Barnes envies the freedom of the layperson: "Parishioners are freed by a spiritual anonymity pastors will never know. Best of all, they're free to tell the old ladies with thin lips that they can take a flying leap if they complain one more time. Pastors have none of these freedoms, and they resent that so much of their individuality was lost on the day of their ordinations."[7]

But does it need to be this way? Is this how the apostles and the early church experienced the household of faith and exercised spiritual leadership? Barnes loves the church. There is no doubt about it. He is an insightful, winsome communicator of the gospel. He is a wise and humble church leader—one of our best. He has devoted his life to helping people experience Christ's peace. Barnes is more than willing to pay the high cost of "crowded loneliness." He insists that this distinction between pastor and people has nothing to do with ego or power, but everything to do with the pastor's vocational

---

7    M. Craig Barnes, *The Pastor as Minor Poet: Texts and Subtexts in the Ministerial* (Grand Rapids: Eerdmans, 2009), 6.

responsibility. "This is the uniqueness of the ordination to Word and Sacrament," he writes. "It has nothing to do with hierarchy and everything to do with the different apportionment of gifts. The cherished Reformation doctrine of the priesthood of all believers does not mean that we are all the same. It means that we are all called to fulfill our mission to live in Christ in the places where we have been called to serve him."[8] However, I question whether we are laboring under a false burden.

Only the pastor, Barnes believes, can "delve into the soul of the congregation in search of holy mysteries."[9] For Barnes the uniqueness of the pastor's vowed commitment distances him from the congregation he serves. "This is what pastors really mean when they complain about the loneliness of their calling," Barnes writes. "No one can do this priestly work for them, or even with them. It is ironic that a profession that surrounds pastors with so many people leaves them alone with their own ponderings. And this is the part of the profession that is completely missed by everyone the pastor serves. . . . The pastor is forced to make the solitary journey into the Holy of Holies to offer exhausted prayers over a cup of tea. There is nothing hierarchical or elitist about this loneliest dimension of the job."[10]

The work that Barnes attributes to the pastor *alone* is the work that the New Testament attributes to the body of Christ *together*. There is no way that one person can or should do everything Barnes insists the pastor should do. We just don't have such a one-sided pastoral description of responsibility and authority in the New Testament. The traditional model that has been reinforced over time through institutional religion is bound to leave the pastor feeling alone and trapped.

Led by the Spirit of Christ the apostles envisioned a very different kind of church. They sought the freedom to know and be known as consonant with the freedom to serve in love and truthfulness.

---

8  Barnes, *The Pastor as Minor Poet*, 61.
9  Barnes, *The Pastor as Minor Poet*, 62.
10  Barnes, *The Pastor as Minor Poet*, 108.

Barnes's description of congregational anonymity and pastoral loneliness is true of many churches. Undoubtedly many pastors can identify with it. But to conform our pastoral theology to the cultural Christianity of institutional religion is neither necessary nor inevitable. We need pastors who lead, certainly. However, assuming authority and humility in a passion for Christ and a love for the household of faith and laboring to preach the whole counsel of God and to offer biblical spiritual direction does not exclude pastors from also receiving within the fellowship of the body of Christ.

Of all people, pastors should make good friends. The reason Jesus gave for calling his disciples friends instead of servants was that he had confided in them. Servants don't know the master's business; they simply do their master's bidding. But Jesus affirmed that friends know what's going on. There is an implicit trust between friends as they experience life together. The matrix of friendship is companionship and conversation. In a nonhierarchical, open, informal, spontaneous way, friends confide in one another, trust, and depend on one another. There is a natural, organic development to friendship that leads to deep feelings of responsibility and intimacy. There is no formula for achieving this, but faithfulness to the commands of Jesus makes friendship possible. There is no better expression of true friendship than to share with a friend everything God has given you.

I confess that I should have done a better job teaching a biblical theology of the household of faith in the churches I've served. When I left my pastoral responsibilities in San Diego for a teaching position in a seminary in Birmingham, my wife Virginia stayed behind to sell our house and organize our move. On the first Sunday I was away she naturally went to church—the church where we worshiped for fourteen years. After the worship service, an elder came to her and asked her, "Why are *you* back? You don't belong here anymore. Your presence here will only confuse people." Virginia was surprised but calmly explained that this is where she worshiped and where her friends were. Unexpectedly, she learned in the weeks that followed that she had two sets of friends: those who had related to her all these years because she was the pastor's wife, and those who related to her because she was their friend. Transactional friendship is a product of a Christendom model of pastoral theology; transformative friendship is the fruit of the gospel-centered household of faith.

## A TWO-WAY STREET

One big difference between a pastoral theology tied to Christendom and a pastoral theology rooted in the household of faith is the necessity of mutuality and friendship. The one-way challenge may be a constant pastoral battle, but it can be faced and overcome by the Spirit of Christ. Good preaching, solid biblical theology, and the shared commitment of the body of Christ are all required to pull off genuine mutuality. We cannot devote ourselves to the teaching of the apostles, the fellowship of brothers and sisters in Christ, to Eucharistic worship, and to prayer, alone. Our culture's individualism and private spirituality meets its match in the household of faith. In order to be faithful and fruitful, pastors need more than mentors; they need the priesthood of all believers.

Good friends, who give as much or more than they receive, have always been a part of my pastoral ministry. Many have reached out to me over the years with encouragement, support, mentorship, and challenge, even as I have served as their pastor. Gifted laypeople have always played a key role in my life and in the life of the church. They have taught, counseled, preached, managed, and administered the church in very effective ways. I have made a point of asking these co-laborers to take on tasks for which I thought they were especially well suited. I am no longer surprised when I see them accomplish these tasks more effectively than I could have.

At a small pastor's conference with about twenty-five pastors, the speaker, a seminary professor and pastor, asked the pastors present, "Who is your pastor?" He went on to relay that one of the assignments he used to give to his seminary students was to ask them to ask their own pastors, "Who is your pastor?" The responses his students received from pastors, however, were so discouraging that he decided to drop the assignment. Most of the pastors interviewed by students lamented a lack of friendship and confessed that they had no one to pastor them.

Good pastors encourage brothers and sisters in Christ to live out the gospel, to express their gifts, and to take on essential responsibilities in the church and in the world. Early in my ministry I didn't always think that way. I did the work myself. But over time I saw the wisdom of sharing the load, depending on others, and genuinely enjoying a "partnership in the gospel" (Phil. 1:5).

There are so many people and opportunities that I could share, but two come to mind that meant a great deal to me. At our church in San Diego we had two Sunday morning services with church school, or Sunday school, in between. After the early service, I often asked one or two members—maybe an elder or a teenager or a student home from university—to walk down the street with me to Starbucks and critique the sermon. I'd ask them: What was helpful in the sermon? What did you find unhelpful? What worked? What was confusing? How could I make the message clearer? The conversations didn't always focus on the mechanics of the sermon, but I really benefitted from these fifteen- to twenty-minute interactions, and they often led to changes for the better in the sermon during the second service.

When I was a pastor in San Diego our church was asked to minister to a family who had flown from Hawaii to San Diego to receive specialized care for their newborn baby who was seriously ill. I reached out to Lori Meals, a neonatal intensive care nurse. Because of Lori's years of experience with gravely ill children and her spiritual maturity, I asked her to help befriend this family and to minister to them. Lori became a special pastor to them, sharing Christ's love with them, praying for them, and helping them through what became for all involved a horrendous ordeal. When she was with the family, she laid aside her normal ministry as a nurse and became their pastor—a pastor with a helpful medical background.

At the outset of my ministry, I doubt if I would have thought of asking Lori to pastor this family. She had her job and I had mine. Even if I had been pulled in twenty different directions, I would have felt it was my responsibility as "the pastor" to be there for this family and everyone else in our congregation facing a crisis. Yet Lori's spiritual depth and willingness to be used made her a natural fit for this challenging responsibility. There were times throughout the year that I felt guilty for asking her to undertake such a difficult ministry. The daily challenges were great, but each time we discussed the situation she assured me that she felt called to help this family. I had not given her this task; the Lord had.

C. S. Lewis pictures friends standing side by side, with their eyes looking ahead. Friendship "must be about something," Lewis observes. "The very condition of having friends is that we should want something else besides friends. . . . Those who have nothing can share nothing; those who are going nowhere can have no fellow-travelers."[11] The story behind our relational life is similar to the truth behind our salvation.[12] In a very real sense we do not make friends—we receive friends. Friendship is a gift. Divine providence is the blessing of God's great faithfulness going before us, conducting the symphony, weaving the tapestry, supervising the project, writing the poetry that we call life. We can rest secure in our friendship with God and in the wisdom that he has shared with us. Building friendships is not a performance-driven human achievement but a slow work of God's grace. Lewis writes:

> A secret Master of the Ceremonies has been at work. Christ, who said to the disciples, "You have not chosen me, but I have chosen you," can truly say to every group of Christian friends, "You have not chosen one another but I have chosen you for one another." The Friendship is not a reward for our discrimination and good taste in

---

11  C. S. Lewis, *The Four Loves* (New York: Harcourt, Brace, 1960), 66–67.
12  See Webster, *Soulcraft*, 83.

finding one another out. It is the instrument by which God reveals to each the beauties of all the others.[13]

## LIFE TOGETHER

Dietrich Bonhoeffer wrote *Life Together* in 1938 for the Confessing Church's illegal, clandestine seminary, to guide twenty-five young pastors. His countercultural vision for Christian community challenged German Christendom and its capitulation to Hitler and Nazism. *Life Together*, though, is a guide to unlearn Christendom in the present day. Bonhoeffer begins by quoting Psalm 133:1: "Behold, how good and how pleasant it is for brethren to dwell together in unity!"[14] He underscores that Christian community is a gift not to be taken for granted. He writes that the Christian "comes to others only through Jesus Christ" who is the singular source of salvation and righteousness.[15] This community, then, is a "divine reality," not a human ideal. He specifies further that Christians come together "as bringers of the message of salvation,"[16] noting that "the physical presence of other Christians is a source of incomparable joy and strength to the believer."[17] In a final condemnation of the structures and aims of Christendom, Bonhoeffer warns that "one who wants more than what Christ has established does not want Christian brotherhood."[18]

The spiritual reality of this community is based on "the clear, manifest Word of God in Jesus Christ," rather than the "dark, turbid urges and desires of the human mind."[19] For Bonhoeffer, life together is centered in Christ. Christians learn to pray the Psalms, understand the Bible, sing in unison, and pray together. They know

---

13   Lewis, *The Four Loves*, 89.
14   Dietrich Bonhoeffer, *Life Together* (San Francisco: HarperCollins, 1954), 17.
15   Bonhoeffer, *Life Together*, 23.
16   Bonhoeffer, *Life Together*, 23.
17   Bonhoeffer, *Life Together*, 19.
18   Bonhoeffer, *Life Together*, 26.
19   Bonhoeffer, *Life Together*, 31.

the hospitality of the kitchen table and the Lord's Supper. They take responsibility for the community and fulfill those responsibilities; they know how to forgive one another.

The spiritual life of individual believers is held in tension with the life of the whole community. The transformation of the community of believers is never sacrificed for the sake of the individual, nor is the individual sacrificed for the sake of community. What is good for the individual is good for the body, and what is good for the body is good for the individual. Members are aware of their motives for solitude and for fellowship: "Let him who cannot be alone beware of community," and "let him who is not in community beware of being alone."[20] Personal solitude, including meditation on the Bible, prayer, and intercession, is necessary to prepare for the combat with evil waged in community. In *Life Together*, Bonhoeffer makes clear that all Christians are called to the ministry of meekness, the ministry of listening, the ministry of helpfulness, the ministry of bearing burdens, the ministry of proclaiming the Word, and the ministry of authority. The truly remarkable achievement of *Life Together* is that, although it was written to pastors, it applies to the priesthood of all believers.

---

20   Bonhoeffer, *Life Together*, 77.

# CHAPTER 5

# A HOLY PRIESTHOOD

*The business model typically assigns to the pastor sole authority, as the CEO of an institution with a board of directors (generally called elders or deacons) whose ecclesiology is often marked more by the values of the* Wall Street Journal *than by the letters of Paul.*

—Joseph Hellerman

The late Eugene Peterson admits to growing up with "a rather severe case of anticlericalism." He had little liking "for professionalism in matters of religion" and he was turned off by "even a whiff of pomposity."[1] There was little danger, Peterson writes of himself, of becoming "a bureaucrat in the time-management business for God or a librarian cataloguing timeless truths."[2] But the danger persists for many seminarians and pastors. Medieval religious traditions and modern business models conspire against the New Testament practice of pastoral ministry in the household of faith. The pastor's heart is vulnerable to professionalism and pomposity and after a few years of "ministry," he may wish that he had pursued an MBA instead

---

1    Peterson, *The Pastor*, 2.
2    Peterson, *The Pastor*, 8.

of an MDiv. The widespread practice of setting up the Father's house of prayer as an enterprise that showcases business skills is something that we have to unlearn.

## A PASTOR'S HEART

Paul Tripp poses a question, "Is it possible that we have constructed a kind of relationship of the pastor to his congregation that cannot work?"[3] In *Dangerous Calling*, Tripp argues that for years he, like many other pastors, unwittingly constructed patterns of thinking and behaving that worked against the church being the church. Tradition, religious habits, and egos conspired to shape the pastor in ways never intended by the New Testament. Tripp admits he fell into the trap described by Peterson: he ran himself and his church like "a bureaucrat in the time management business for God."[4]

Eventually, he came to lament his fixation with "staffing, strategic plans, building programs, financial planning, corporate structures, audience demographics, cultural relevance, career advancement, budget maintenance, resourcing initiatives, etc."[5] He learned the hard way that our culture "does not offer congenial conditions in which to live vocationally as a pastor."[6] Tripp became convinced that the heart of the matter is the pastor's heart:

> The fundamental battle of pastoral ministry is not with the shifting values of the surrounding culture. It is not the struggle with resistant people who don't seem to esteem the gospel. It is not the fight for the success of the ministries of the church. And it is not the constant struggle of resources and personnel to accomplish the mission. No, the war of the pastorate is a deeply personal war. It

---

3    Peterson, *The Pastor*, 69.
4    Peterson, *The Pastor*, 8.
5    Paul David Tripp, *Dangerous Calling: Confronting the Unique Challenges of Pastoral Ministry* (Wheaton, IL: Crossway, 2012), 218.
6    Peterson, *The Pastor*, 4.

is fought on the ground of the pastor's heart. It is a war
of values, allegiances, and motivations. It is about subtle
desires and foundational dreams. This war is the greatest
threat to every pastor. Yet it is a war that we often naively
ignore or quickly forget in the busyness of local-church
ministry.[7]

Tripp explores the "disconnect between the public pastoral persona
and the private" self in "many, many pastors' lives."[8] He experienced
"a huge disconnect" between his "private persona" and his outwardly
successful pastoral ministry. At home he admits he was irritable, impatient, and difficult to live with, but at church he was the "gracious
and patient pastor."[9] His pastoral success went to his head. He no
longer thought of himself "as a child of God, in daily need of grace."
He prided himself on being a winning pastor, worthy of privilege
and praise. However, he confesses that his success was more in his
mind than in reality.[10] His carefully constructed pastoral persona
was false, and it fueled his pride and led to isolation and loneliness.
The church needed him, he imagined. He didn't need the church.

Tripp believes his "heart problem" began in seminary. "I am
convinced," he writes, "that the crisis of pastoral culture often begins
in the seminary class. It begins with a distant, impersonal, infor-
mation-based handling of the Word of God. It begins with pastors
who, in their seminary years, became quite comfortable with holding
God's Word distant from their own hearts."[11] In seminary he felt dis-
connected from meaningful communion with God, and this carried
over into his pastoral ministry. It "was all shockingly impersonal,"
he writes. "It was about theological content, exegetical rightness,
ecclesiastical commitments, and institutional advancement. It was
about preparing for the next sermon, getting the next meeting agenda

---

7   Tripp, *Dangerous Calling*, 98.
8   Tripp, *Dangerous Calling*, 21.
9   Tripp, *Dangerous Calling*, 18.
10  Tripp, *Dangerous Calling*, 23.
11  Tripp, *Dangerous Calling*, 52.

straight, and filling the requisite leadership openings. It was about budgets, strategic plans, and ministry partnerships."[12]

Eventually, after a lot of soul-searching, Tripp scrapped the aloof, professional, know-it-all business model forged in seminary and began to pursue a healthier pastoral ministry. He went back to the New Testament to better understand the fellowship of believers and pastoral ministry. He reflected on a number of biblical passages that underscore the essential ministry of the whole body of Christ to all believers, including pastors (see Heb. 3:12–13; Eph. 4:11–16; 1 Cor. 12:14–25; Col. 3:15–17). A serious study of the early church and her spiritual leaders revolutionized his outlook on the church and pastoral ministry.

Now Tripp encourages pastors to belong to small groups, not as leaders but as ordinary believers. He encourages pastors to have spiritual mentors in their lives who hold them accountable. He advocates "appropriate self-disclosure" in sermons and plenty of "family-to-family" hospitality.[13] He sums it up this way: "It really is an 'all-of-God's-people-all-of-the-time' paradigm."[14] He adds, "I now know that I need to commit myself to living in intentionally intrusive, Christ-centered, grace-driven, redemptive community."[15]

As Tripp's story highlights, the inner life of the pastor is of fundamental importance. The theological and structural issues of the Christendom model, however, make it difficult for pastors to attend to their inner life and offer the leadership and spiritual formation envisioned by the New Testament. The tradition of a special call to the ministry isolates the pastor within himself. Success or failure rides on the assurance that the minister has been called.

Church of Scotland pastor William Still (1911–1997) epitomizes what many believe is the only way to think about the pastoral ministry. He writes, "The key is the Call. If you are not absolutely sure

---

12  Tripp, *Dangerous Calling*, 63.
13  Tripp, *Dangerous Calling*, 79–82.
14  Tripp, *Dangerous Calling*, 91.
15  Tripp, *Dangerous Calling*, 84.

or cannot come soon to absolute assurance that God has laid His hand upon you for this work—flee it."[16] This notion of a singular male pastor sounds spiritual, but sadly this classical tradition is actually foreign to the New Testament. Still writes, "If the hope of the world is Christ . . . that hope can only be fulfilled by men pouring out the riches of Christ's saving grace upon the Lord's people through the Scriptures." Still implies that everything rides on the pastor's preaching. This prompts him to dispense advice in authoritarian and absolute terms: "No one should be a minister if he can be anything else in the world." Or, "Don't be a minister if you can help it. It is the worst job in the world. But it is also the best." Still's conviction that "only a comparatively small proportion of those who go forward to the ministry are really called of God" sows seeds of doubt and consternation in the mind of struggling pastors.[17] Still's classic model of pastoral ministry insists on an isolating singularity: "If you are called of God, you are not your own, and you are certainly not your wife's, nor your children's, nor even your congregation's. Keep close to God, there is no substitute for that. Others may give you advice, but unless they are in the same position of waiting in holy fear before the God of all the earth, the God of their calling, their advice is not worth having. Don't assume that God will tell another what you should do."[18] The approach to pastoral ministry envisioned by William Still separates the pastor from his family and his congregation. It isolates him as the pivotal means of ministry for *his* flock. The whole concept is foreign to the New Testament household of faith, which describes a plurality of Spirit-gifted leaders, mutual submission, and a priesthood of all believers.

The heart of the pastor is important, but the state of his heart, in part, depends on the structural dynamics of the household of faith. This is why pastoral identity and congregational identity

---

16  William Still, *The Work of the Pastor* (Ross-shire, UK: Christian Focus, 2001), 113.

17  Still, *The Work of the Pastor*, 113–14.

18  Still, *The Work of the Pastor*, 117–18.

deserve to be in a dynamic relationship within the household of faith. We cannot work on the pastor's identity apart from the congregation's identity.

## CHURCH STRUCTURES

New Testament scholar and co-pastor Joseph Hellerman challenges the prevailing organizational and leadership models shaping pastoral ministry. Hellerman writes, "I do not wish to minimize the personal responsibility of persons who leverage authority in hurtful ways.... Each of us will answer for the ways we lead people. This is not a book, however, about the inner life of the Christian leader. It is a book about the institutional structures of our churches, structures that often determine the relational contours of our ministry."[19] Hellerman believes we are ignoring the "values and priorities" of leadership taught and modeled by the apostles. He argues that we have "traded biblical ecclesiology for a secular paradigm of hierarchy and institutionalism." This "approach to congregational life has led all too often to an insecure, narcissistic leader acquiring unilateral authority over the rest of the community."[20]

Hellerman notes that the early church evolved amid the Roman Empire, a highly stratified society. Social class distinctions in clothing and rank were significant in this Greco-Roman honor-seeking culture. "Persons in Mediterranean antiquity vigorously competed with one another for honor and social status in the public arena." He argues that when the early church took root, it resisted this social stratification and these hierarchical organizational patterns. The apostles "intentionally subverted the relational values of the dominant culture, where power, status, and the exercise of authority were concerned."[21]

---

19  Joseph H. Hellerman, *Embracing Shared Ministry: Power and Status in the Early Church and Why It Matters Today* (Grand Rapids: Kregel, 2013), 17.
20  Hellerman, *Embracing Shared Ministry*, 292.
21  Hellerman, *Embracing Shared Ministry*, 52–53.

Using the church at Philippi as an example, Hellerman describes the sociological impact of the gospel: "Paul's goal was to create a very different kind of community among the followers of Jesus in first-century Philippi. The Philippian church was to be a community that discouraged competition for status and privilege, a place where the honor game was off-limits, in summary, a community in which persons with power and authority used their social capital not to further their own personal or familial agendas but, rather, to serve their brothers and sisters in Christ."[22] In other words, the gospel led not only to personal salvation but to social salvation. The most profound relational reconciliation and sociological realignment ever imagined took place at this time. The early church and the apostles demonstrated that one cannot be a new creation in Christ, individually, without belonging to a radically new community formed in Christ.

The apostle Paul, in his letter to the believers at Ephesus, laid out the most profound relational reconciliation and sociological realignment ever imagined. From the depths of human depravity, we are raised in Christ to the heights of salvation (Eph. 2:1–10), and from the hostility of human enmity, we are delivered by the peace of Christ into the household of God (Eph. 2:11–22). In Christ, the unbridgeable chasm between God and humankind is bridged and the irreconcilable differences between humans themselves are reconciled in Christ.

It is not only a *personal* conversion of the believer's heart and mind, then, but it is a *social* conversion of the believer's entire life. We cannot be a new creation in Christ without belonging to the new community in Christ.[23] As a concrete, sociological body, the church was meant to be "a sign and proof of a change that affects the institutions and structures, patterns and spans of the bodily and

---

22  Hellerman, *Embracing Shared Ministry*, 106.
23  Douglas D. Webster, *The Christ Letter: A Christological Approach to Preaching and Practicing Ephesians* (Eugene, OR: Cascade, 2012), 47.

spiritual, social and individual existence of all humanity."[24] Conversion in the early church meant a lifelong, communal journey that
involved reshaping an entire way of living and system of values.[25]
The gospel demands a fundamental reorientation of beliefs, a reso-
cialization of belonging, and a reformation of behavior.

And yet the sociological changes the gospel demands have always been difficult to institute. Hellerman notes the early Christians
were "marginalized by the pagan majority. Christians in Philippi
would have been almost irresistibly tempted to replicate the ideals
and practices of the dominate culture, by generating in the church
a hierarchy of honors that would mimic the social contours of the
colony at large."[26] However, the gospel calls for a profound break
with existing social patterns of status and stratification. Hellerman
offers practical proof of this apostolic goal in the refusal of both
Paul and Silas to reveal their Roman citizenship at the outset of
their ministry (Acts 16). "Like Jesus, as portrayed in Philippians
2:6–8, Paul and Silas did not consider their status as something to
be exploited but, instead, willingly endured suffering for the benefit
of others." Hellerman sees the parallels between the narrative of
Acts 16 and the story of Jesus celebrated in the early Christ hymn
(Phil. 2:6–11) as not only sociologically significant but indicative
of the early church's cultural strategy.[27]

In light of what the church is always up against, Hellerman
reasons, the relational structure of the household of faith is all
the more important. This structure provides support for the inner
life of the pastor, as well as the rest of the congregation. Instead of
an autonomous, individualistic, and hierarchical organizational
structure, Hellerman proposes an accountable, relational, and col-
laborative structure. "Like the Philippians," Hellerman writes, "we

---

24  Markus Barth, *Ephesians*, The Anchor Yale Bible (New Haven, CT: Yale Uni-
    versity Press, 1974), 1:365.
25  Alan Kreider, *The Change of Conversion: Christian Mission and Modern Cul-
    ture* (Harrisburg, PA: Trinity Press International, 1999), xv.
26  Hellerman, *Embracing Shared Ministry*, 123.
27  Hellerman, *Embracing Shared Ministry*, 116.

need a social context for ministry that is different from the world around us, a way of doing church that will provide the checks and balances necessary for healthy pastoral leadership in our congregations." Hellerman continues: "The pathway back to Jesus-like leadership begins with a plurality of pastor-elders who relate to one another first as family members in Christ, and who function only secondarily—and only within the primary relational context—as vision-casting, decision-making leaders for the broader church family." This he believes will help "recapture Paul's cruciform vision for Christian leadership."[28]

The apostle Paul's vision of the church was marked by the cross and, Hellerman writes, was "anti-Roman to the core." The gospel, more broadly, was anti-Roman to the extent that the prevailing culture was dehumanizing and self-destructive. In this way, the gospel of grace provided a meaningful strategy for human flourishing.[29] Hellerman: "By identifying the church as a family, Paul sought to establish a relational context in which the honor game was no longer acceptable for those who claimed to be followers of Jesus. Instead of competing with each other and grasping for honor, Christians in the colony were to relate like siblings, that is, they were to 'outdo one another in showing honor.'"[30] Hellerman argues that it is "a simple but incontrovertible fact that certain ways of doing church naturally lend themselves to a Jesus-like use of authority on the part of leaders."[31] He concludes, "Christian leadership begins with a group of pastors who share life together, who genuinely love one another, and who lead their church, as a team, out of the richness of the soil of those peer relationships."[32]

Paul Tripp is right when he says that the heart of the matter is the pastor's heart. But Joseph Hellerman is also right when he concludes that how the body of Christ is organized is as essential

---

28   Hellerman, *Embracing Shared Ministry*, 292–93.
29   Hellerman, *Embracing Shared Ministry*, 169.
30   Hellerman, *Embracing Shared Ministry*, 192.
31   Hellerman, *Embracing Shared Ministry*, 179.
32   Hellerman, *Embracing Shared Ministry*, 306.

to the health and holiness of the household of faith. The inner life of the pastoral team is crucial to the health of the church, but so is the "outer life," or the structure of the church. Even the sincerest pastor with a heart after God's heart will be crushed by a corporate structure that is modeled after the world. As important as personal conversion is, the impact of the gospel on our social structures is as indispensable. A biblical understanding of the church means that walls of hostility and division have to come down. Social stratification and worldly status seeking need to be challenged and upended. An interdependent body, an every-member ministry, and humble, authoritative spiritual leadership deserve to be *instituted*. Pastoral theology concerns the heart and the relational and organizational structure of the church.

Pastoral authority is important. It is rooted in a Christ-centered life, biblical wisdom, godly character, personal integrity, spiritual gifts, and prayerful discernment. It should not be established by setting up a person in a position or in an office, and declaring, "You're the boss." There is a difference between running a business, coaching a sports team, commanding an army, and guiding the household of faith. Christendom leadership is worldly leadership based on individual initiative, institutional power, and personal charisma. In the household of faith, pastoral authority and guidance requires mutual submission in Christ. It is a group project and a team effort. It is a joint venture that requires a plurality of gifted, respected, godly men and women. Pastors and elders serve under the headship of Christ and, in turn, they faithfully and fruitfully "equip his people for works of service, so that the body of Christ may be built up until we all reach unity in the faith and in the knowledge of the Son of God and become mature, attaining to the whole measure of the fullness of Christ" (Eph. 4:12–13).

In my first church as a full-time lead pastor, I followed the founding pastor who, by all accounts, was an excellent pastor. He faithfully and effectively served Christ in that congregation for thirty years. However, by the end of my second year the church was in turmoil, and it seemed that I was the cause of much of the frustration and anger. There were a few factions in the church that liked very little about me or my work. Older members were grieving the loss of their dearly loved pastor, and I didn't fit the bill. Others were upset that I wasn't warm and personable. We had just come from eleven years in Toronto, and apparently my demeanor rubbed small-town Midwestern sensibilities in the wrong way. Still others found fault with my sermons. They were too intellectual, too theological, and not evangelistic enough. I needed to lighten up and tell a few jokes. I'm sure there was some truth behind all these criticisms. I had a lot to learn about pastoral ministry. But I was earnestly trying to be a good pastor. I was not, as some thought, trying to offend them.

As all this criticism was heating up and wearing me down, one of the older members suggested that the elders call a town meeting so everyone could air their grievances. Thinking that maybe this would clear the air so we could get on with the ministry, I naively went along with the idea. That was a big mistake. Seventy-five people showed up with notes in hand, ready to do battle. We put chairs in a circle, and I was positioned in the middle. For more than an hour I attempted to answer a barrage of criticisms, covering every aspect of my pastoral work. After all these years I don't recall specific criticisms, but I remember hot, red faces, a lot of angry rhetoric, and the group's visceral frustration *with me*. I was looking into the faces and hearing the voices of the same people I worshiped with every Sunday morning and evening. It felt and still feels like an out-of-body experience.

I knew after that evening that I was not the new full-time pastor but their transition pastor, an interim, whom no one thought they needed. It was the beginning of the end. There was too much hostility from some and too much apathy in others for us to stay and have a meaningful ministry. There were individuals who were supportive and encouraging of my ministry, but they remained silent that night. They were passive observers of a church train wreck. When we departed a year later, they complained that our leaving was a betrayal. We were all operating, pastor and people alike, from a misguided notion that the pastor was set apart and set above the congregation to fend for himself. I stood alone, pressed to represent my work, and without the support of elders or deacons. I promised myself that night that I would never face a setup like that again. I would never go it alone again.

Pastoral authority is not a one-man show. It is rooted in the shared solidarity of the people of God. In the tradition of the early church a plurality of pastors belongs to a team of gifted, committed, godly men and women. In the household of faith, pastors should never stand alone. The lonely, isolated, pastor ought to be a relic of the past.

Years later I was invited back to this church to preach. I was greeted as a long-lost favorite son by some of the very same people who criticized my ministry and wanted me to leave. I genuinely enjoyed seeing them again. In the providence of God, if I had been further along on the unlearning curve, I might have stayed. If I knew then what I know now about shared leadership in the household of faith, I might have endured the criticism and worked for change.

## THE NARCISSISTIC PASTOR

"I'm not sure I can hang in there much longer," said the voice over the phone. "Do you have time to talk?" Later that afternoon Ben came over we talked. He was struggling with what it meant to be a pastor and questioning his role on the pastoral team for a large evangelical church. He had spent the last several years serving as the right-hand man to an evangelical senior pastor who had made sweeping changes in the life of the church. Loyalty required Ben to take "a lot of hits" for the pastor. Every week he spent literally hours defending the pastor to church members who complained that the senior pastor was indifferent to their perspectives. Ben was loyal and on board with the "vision," but when the senior pastor hired a young pastor as a director over him, he no longer felt like he was in the inner circle. Nothing changed in Ben's job description, but his access to the senior pastor, who was seldom at church during the week, was limited.

When a capable, hard-working member of the staff, who reported directly to Ben, was let go without warning, Ben was especially upset. The senior pastor's report to the board of elders only made matters worse, because he stated that Ben knew all about the termination and supported it. Ben wanted to challenge the senior pastor in the meeting, but he knew the pastor would take it negatively. The next day Ben spoke to him about it in private. But as he feared, the senior pastor dismissed his concerns as nitpicky and small-minded. He chided Ben to keep the big picture in view. Ben left the meeting feeling bewildered and bullied. He had worked for the pastor for four years, but he began to wonder if he really knew the man, or if anyone did.

Ben was now experiencing firsthand what many members had complained to him about. He had defended the pastor faithfully, but now he was recalling the numerous conversations he had with faithful members who said that it was a waste of time to talk to the pastor. Many of these members, even long-standing members, ended up leaving the church. Their common lament was that the senior pastor only cared about his own agenda and that he used people as a means to achieve his own goals. Ben honestly liked the pastor's preaching, but he was having trouble reconciling the pastor's positive public persona and his behind-the-scenes maneuvering.

A number of further actions, however, confirmed for Ben the pastor's struggle with narcissism. At the last board meeting before the start of summer, the pastor arranged for his three favorite elders to make three motions: first, to suspend elder meetings for the summer; second, to grant the pastor an annual three-month sabbatical; and third, to increase his salary to help pay for travel expenses during his sabbatical.

Subsequently, a bewildered couple told Ben that they met with the pastor because they were having marriage difficulties. The pastor suggested that they needed to go to R-rated movies to build sexual excitement in their marriage. They said the pastor never opened the Bible and never prayed with them, and they confessed that he made them feel funny for seeking help.

Another new member sought Ben's counsel after the senior pastor approached him to set up a meeting with his wealthy, out-of-state father who was known to be a billionaire. Before this request, the new parishioner had never talked with the pastor. Understandably, the new member felt the request was inappropriate. But the pastor persisted, and the new member reluctantly agreed to set up a thirty-minute phone conversation with his father. He told Ben that the senior pastor talked with his father for more than an hour. The pastor had explained his need for a private pastoral retreat home in California. He was not shy about soliciting the billionaire's funding to make it happen.

We don't need to look too hard in the Bible to find the classic narcissist. King Saul fits the profile. There were moments when the king led the people of Israel with genuine humility and charismatic power, but over the course of his career, and especially when he felt threatened, it became increasingly evident that Saul suffered from what we presently call narcissistic personality disorder (NPD). While the label is new, the disorder is rooted in human depravity and has been around since time immemorial.

The ancient Greek fable of Narcissus describes a sixteen-year-old boy who was so handsome that he attracted people to himself, but he could not relate to them and love them back. He was too in love with his own image. He was so transfixed by his own reflection in a pond that he lay down next to the pond and pined away for the image of himself. Narcissus represents the self-focused person who has a deep hunger for inordinate praise, along with powerful feelings of superiority and entitlement, and a strong reaction to rejection or disapproval. The narcissist is incapable of real empathy and self-examination and uses people for his or her own ends.

King Saul is a classic case of narcissism. Under pressure, King Saul acted unilaterally and assumed responsibilities that did not belong to him. Out of fear, he usurped the authority of the prophet Samuel and reacted recklessly (1 Sam. 13:7–14). He demanded unreasonable loyalty from his subjects and threatened family members when they did not comply with his self-serving dictates (1 Sam. 14:24–45). He congratulated himself by setting up a monument in his own honor and bragged that he had carried out the Lord's instructions even though he had blatantly violated the expressed will of God (1 Sam. 15:12–13). He reacted with suspicion and paranoia when his faithful and loyal coworkers appeared to be more successful than he was (1 Sam. 18:6–9). Saul was obsessed with retaining power so that even when David proved his absolute loyalty to Saul, as the Lord's anointed, he could not stop hating David and seeking to kill him (1 Sam. 24:5–7; 26:8–25). In the end, fear drove Saul to take his own life (1 Sam. 27:1–25; 31:1–6).

Saul's leadership lacked genuine obedience and suffered from plenty of spiritual-sounding talk. Undoubtedly, his own self-serving rationalizations justified waging war against those closest to him, but Saul's greatest conflict was the battle within himself. This is the war that nearly drove him insane. He was driven by fear, deep insecurities, and a highly inflated ego. He became his own worst enemy.

Pride is a chronic temptation for pastors. Many pastors suffer from narcissistic tendencies that, if allowed to go unchecked, can wreak havoc in our lives and in the household of faith. We are tempted to take off the full armor of God and take up the weapons of the world. These are the spiritual and relational ego battles that we fight out of fear and pride. These are the battles we fight because of the war within us. Saul may be an extreme example of NPD, but he is not alone.

I recall a veteran associate pastor sharing his experience with a suspected narcissistic senior pastor. Here's a paraphrase of his description:

> The NPD pastor creates a culture in which nontransparent communication is the norm. He thrives on rumor and gossip, even as he preaches vehemently against such evils. He seeks to control the communication flow by creating confusion as to what is private and confidential and what is public knowledge. Triangulation, the habit

of not communicating openly and honestly face to face
between two people but communicating through a third
party, is a common relational tactic.

Congregations that have an NPD leader will system-
atically lose good people because they sense the negative
undercurrent running through the staff and congregation. People leave quietly to get away from the sick (and
ultimately dying) congregation. The pastoral staff and lay
leaders will not follow up with these retreating members
because they know why people are leaving. Meanwhile,
the NPD pastor will fawn over new members and try to
create a buffer zone of support from his loyal following.

The pain generated by a narcissist is hard to calculate and the
damage done to believers is virtually impossible to measure. The
disruption, manipulation, intimidation, miscommunication,
and constant power plays can blend with the pastor's powerful
preaching, sanctimonious prayers, and public charisma. The pastor
endears himself to those who praise him and undermines anyone
who dares question him. If it became known that the senior pastor
was having an affair or embezzling church funds, the elders would
know what they needed to do, but the narcissistic pastor poses a far
more difficult and slippery issue. The diagnosis is difficult to make,
because the narcissist never sees it, and no medication or time off
is going to fix it. Nothing short of radical repentance in the spirit
of Psalm 51 will redeem the situation and the person.

The contrasting picture of Saul and David in the biblical narrative exposes Saul as a narcissist and highlights the character of a
person after God's own heart. Saul was driven by fear; David was
driven by the fear of the Lord. And even though David sinned terri-
bly, he turned to God in deep dependence and heartfelt repentance.
Saul was mastered by the sovereign self. David was anointed by
the Spirit of the Lord. A paranoid Saul fought his own battles and
waged war against his own demons, while David depended on the
Lord to save him. He acknowledged that "the battle is the Lord's"

(1 Sam. 17:47). David, the shepherd king and miserable sinner, was saved by grace.

Jesus Christ, however, is the one who models perfectly and, further, empowers cruciform leadership in the body of Christ. He spoke plainly, "You know that the rulers of the Gentiles lord it over them, and their high officials exercise authority over them. Not so with you. Instead, whoever wants to become great among you must be your servant, and whoever wants to be first must be your slave—just as the Son of Man did not come to be served, but to serve, and to give his life as a ransom for many" (Matt. 20:25–28). Jesus made the connection explicit. Serving and suffering belong together. True Christ-honoring leadership has its roots in his atoning sacrifice. This is where leadership begins and ends.

God-centered humility and self-sacrifice are key to replacing the hubris and self-centeredness inherent in the narcissistic pastor. Narcissism usually indicates deep and unresolved issues of self-worth and shame. The first step in dealing with a narcissistic pastor requires his or her removal from power; the second step is to offer spiritual direction and counseling. Power is to the narcissist what narcotics are to the addict.

Removing a narcissistic pastor from office is difficult because there is no obvious moral failure: no sexual affair or bank account to use as evidence. Nevertheless, a consistent pattern of manipulation, deception, and duplicity over time requires action by the spiritual leaders of the church. Churches that turn to outside experts for reconciliation only complicate matters and put off the inevitable. The danger here is to obscure the real issue by blaming the church culture, when, in fact, it is a single individual who has corrupted the leadership of the church. Leaders who have been supportive of the pastor and discounted the concerns of members and staff will be especially slow to act. This face-saving inertia must be overcome in order for the church to heal. If leaders hide behind a third party, they will only do more harm to the church.

The church should also examine the expectations and roles we associate with pastoral ministry. Self-centeredness is inherent in all of us, but the modern American pastorate seems especially susceptible to narcissism. There is plenty of work to be done if we are serious about pursuing a biblical understanding of the household of faith in Christ. Jesus meant for us to practice the priesthood of all believers, every-member ministry, shared leadership, and the gifts of the Spirit. If we expect our pastors to be men and women after God's own heart, they will have to be saved from themselves and also from our worldly expectations.

## GOSPEL CLARITY

The structures of Christendom come with baggage: spiritual anonymity, crowded loneliness, cultural accommodation, religious individualism, a private faith, big endowments, spiritual syncretism, and pastors with inflated egos. These churches reflect the spirit of the times—its wealth, prestige, professionalism, and ethical conventions. Like any other large organization, these institutions prevail by virtue of their power, wealth, and status. The line between the admirers of Jesus and the followers of Jesus is fuzzy at best. Pastors are tasked with "running the church," and they are beholden to budgets, donors, and powerful personalities. It makes sense that a pastoral theology that serves Christendom will not serve the household of faith. The Christendom religion produces nice people who believe in themselves. They love their church the way they love a club or favorite sports team. The structures of Christendom serve to conform worshippers to the culture rather than facilitate their transformation in the Spirit of Christ.

The household of faith is rooted in the New Testament, and, like the early church, she is forced to wage war on two fronts: the religious and the secular. The transformative power of the gospel creates "one new humanity" and this one race is commissioned with a global mission. We remain resident aliens in our home culture, even as we are adopted into a new global family. We are God's people, encompassing "every nation, tribe, people, and language" (Rev. 7:9). In Christ, we are this third race—holy ones, members of God's household, and joined together to become a holy temple. The New Testament describes the church as "like living stones" that "are being built into a spiritual house to be a holy priesthood, offering spiritual sacrifices acceptable to God through Jesus Christ" (1 Peter 2:5).

Missiologist Timothy Tennent describes the clarity of the household of faith and the fog of Christendom this way:

> When you walk into a vibrant church, you can immediately sense the difference. At every point, you meet gospel clarity. The church exudes confidence in the unique work of Jesus Christ. They understand the power and authority of God's Word. They feel the lostness of the world and the urgency to bring the good news to everyone. At every point, you observe gospel clarity. . . . You can actually sense the presence of Christ in your midst. . . . In contrast, when you walk into the churches in decline you are immediately brought into "the Fog." What is the fog? It is the inability to be clear about anything. There is no clarity about who Jesus Christ is and what He has done. There is no clarity about the Scriptures as the authoritative Word of God. There is no clarity about the urgency to reach the lost. . . . In the "fog," Jesus Christ is just one of many noble teachers in the world."[33]

Maybe this scenario strikes you as too impressionistic, but when the clarity of the gospel blows away the fog, you know the difference.

---

33  Timothy Tennent, "Gospel Clarity vs. 'The Fog,'" *Timothy Tennent* (blog), December 16, 2014, https://timothytennent.com/gospel-clarity-vs-the-fog.

CHAPTER 6

# PASTOR AS SHEPHERD

*Being a pastor that satisfies a congregation is one of the easiest jobs on the face of the earth, if we are satisfied with satisfying congregations.*

—Eugene Peterson

*Since the organization of the Christian church as an institution is so physically real and apparently understandable, I begin to imagine that the most important task for me as a Christian is to manage this institution and to make it succeed for God's purposes. . . . I am organizing the organization and when my own expectations for that organization become too important to me, I have lost the vision of the mystery of God's presence in my own life and among these people who are God's people.*

—Earl Palmer

The New Testament shows little interest in how churches organize and administer their leadership offices. We know that the organization of the early church was simple, shared, and highly relational. Ironically, the modern church is much more top down and male oriented than the early church. Michael Green observes in *Evangelism in the Early Church* that

Christianity "was from its inception a lay movement, and so it continued for a remarkably long time." When the believers were evicted from Jerusalem following Stephen's martyrdom, men and women "went everywhere gossiping the gospel; they did it naturally, enthusiastically, and with the conviction of those who are not paid to say that sort of thing." The absence of a distinction between "full-time ministers and laymen in this responsibility to spread the gospel by every means possible," meant that "everyone was to be an apologist, at least to the extent of being ready to give a good account of the hope that was within them."[1]

When we add a host of managerial tasks to the biblical profile of pastoral ministry, we add to the burden and subtract from the value of pastoral ministry. Tradition assigns these administrative tasks to pastors, but they should not even belong to pastors to delegate, because if everything falls to pastors to supervise and delegate, pastors end up as general managers "running the church." Pastors feel like subcontractors in the Jesus business, constantly trying to recruit and affirm volunteers, to help them run a religious bureaucracy.

## PASTORAL IDENTITY

On one hand, we may want a mayoral pastor, a religious master of ceremonies and managerial supervisor, one who is gifted in the small talk and administration. On the other hand, we want a Protestant priest, one who single-handedly represents the church and mediates God to the world.[2] Whether separately or combined, these two profiles, pastor as people pleaser and pastor as Christ figure, sabotage the ministry of the Word. The apostles and the early church offer an alternative model. What we *should* want in pastors is succinctly and beautifully expressed by the apostle Peter's

---

1   Michael Green, *Evangelism in the Early Church* (Grand Rapids: Eerdmans, 1970), 173–75.
2   See Scot McKnight, *Pastor Paul: Nurturing a Culture of Christoformity in the Church* (Grand Rapids: Brazos, 2019), 9, 21.

description of shepherds at the conclusion of his first letter. All the unlearning curve does is clear away the religious busy work so we can get down to doing the real work of the church.

The traditional understanding of ministry has been narrowly focused upon a few men, rather than upon the body of Christ and the distribution of the gifts of the Spirit among men and women. The burden of authentic ministry was meant to be shared throughout the household of faith. Instead, it became the special responsibility of the pastor. Tradition fostered a dichotomy between spiritual and secular work and reduced most believers to passive spectators, who live out their Christian faith vicariously through their pastor. To counter this way of being the church, we want to encourage the synergistic relationship between pastoral identity and congregational identity. The priesthood of all believers makes pastors; the pastor doesn't make the priesthood of all believers.

## TERMS OF ENDEARMENT

Congregations do not set out to make life impossible for the pastor, but, beginning with the pastoral search process, they often do. No one wants to admit it, but a pastoral search committee is often looking for a little messiah, a forty-year-old experienced pastor with a young family and a bright future. Invariably there are two "job descriptions," one written down on paper and another in the imagination of the committee. Everybody wants an excellent preacher, an efficient chief of staff, a caring pastor, and someone who will attract seekers to their church. The real expectations go unwritten. These unwritten expectations have more to do with a congregation's ego and security needs. Search committees dutifully publish their list of pastoral qualities, but what they really want goes on an unwritten wish list. Congregations tend to hire out of their neediness—their woundedness. When a congregation says that they need a healer—a warm, caring pastor—watch out! More than likely, they can't get along with one another, and their life together is in shambles. Or they are looking for a hero who will make something great of the church. They may not say it in so many words, but they're looking for the "wow" factor.

Regrettably, many pastors find their work all-consuming. Imagine that all of a doctor's patients knew one another, and they gathered weekly to compare notes. Or if all the clients of a lawyer enjoyed potluck suppers together. Imagine the solidarity and synergy of demand, the oppressive nature of accountability, the peculiar power of shared complaints and expectations. It is dangerously easy to subscribe to a philosophy of ministry that demands that the pastor be all things to all people at all times—cheerfully! The doctor-patient relationship is professionally limited to the physical needs of the patient. You wouldn't think of calling your doctor because you can't afford to get your car fixed. Imagine showing up at your doctor's office just to spend time together because you feel your doctor doesn't know you well enough.

The attorney-client relationship is usually limited to the client's legal needs. Lawyers don't usually attend their client's birthday parties, wedding anniversaries, piano recitals, or listen to them as they graphically recount their visit to the doctor, unless of course they are suing their doctor for malpractice. Because he is their pastor, many churchgoers feel there is nothing that their pastor should not be interested in about their lives. He must be interested in them and everything about them.

How can a pastor have a one-on-one relationship with several hundred members and remain sane? But many parishioners believe that this is a reasonable expectation. And many pastors suffer from unrelenting guilt for disappointing the expectations of church members. Pastors get tired of living on a one-way street of on-demand ministry, catering to people who cling to their weakness as a claim to significance, a merit badge that should invite attention and sympathy. Pastors also grow weary of those who cling to their power and wealth and expect attention on the basis of this power and wealth. Neither the worldly weak nor the worldly wealthy has any practical intention of growing in the grace and knowledge of the Lord Jesus Christ, but that doesn't lessen the demands they place on the pastor. These are some of the pressures that shape and distort the pastoral identity.

I have vivid memories of an elder meeting in our Bloomington, Indiana church. Don felt I was wasting my time. I wasn't spending enough time with people, and the people I was spending time with were the wrong people. I was in my late thirties, and, as Paul would say, a "manager of the mysteries God has revealed" for a thriving congregation in a university town. I was working hard, preaching at two services on Sunday morning, and preaching a different sermon at an evening service. Several hundred townspeople and several hundred students came to each service. For forty-six weekends each year I preached two different sermons. Beyond preaching, my week was filled with one-on-one counseling with church members and church administration. We had three young children, and it was easy for me to feel guilty for overworking.

If I was permitted to do it all over again, I would try to change people's perspectives on what it means to belong to the household of faith. We would *unlearn* the habits of tradition, such as the singular, solo responsibilities of the lead pastor in a congregation of passive recipients of spiritual services. But I didn't understand all of this at the time. I was a proverbial deer in the headlights, not a perceptive pastor.

Don was an authority figure in the community and in the church. He was the town building inspector—the only building inspector I knew who wore a badge and a gun to a church board meeting. He and his wife drove yellow Cadillacs with license plates that read "His" and "Hers." Don was particularly upset that I didn't attend his men's Monday morning Bible study, which met at six thirty in the morning. He envisioned the pastor spending a lot of time relating to the townspeople. He was looking for a friendly, mayoral pastor who put everyone at ease, a man who was gifted at small talk and who made people feel important. Sermons were not a big deal for Don. A simple invitation to follow Jesus peppered with amusing anecdotes and congregational encouragement was what Don was looking for in a sermon.

So, one night at a board meeting, late into the meeting, Don pushed back his chair, propped his right leg over his left knee and demanded that I keep a log of my use of my time, hour by hour, for every day of the week. He was serious. I did not know what to say. I felt blindsided. I thought my long hours and hard work were obvious, but apparently counseling university students and "marginal" congregants was not Don's idea of an effective use of my time. He thought I should be socializing with the church's big givers. As Don was complaining that I was not working hard enough, I was thinking that I literally could not work more hours each day. To add to the humiliation of this spontaneous job performance review, none of the elders spoke up on my behalf. Everyone sat still and looked down. As one elder explained to me later, "We pay you the big bucks to handle people like Don." I'm sure he was joking about "the big bucks."

Every response I could think of sounded defensive or petty. I kept my cool outwardly. We ended the meeting soon after, a meeting that had gone on way too long, and I went to my office to wait until everyone left. I couldn't handle anything more. I was angry and upset and ready to quit. When I got in the car, I punched the steering wheel hard—too hard I guess, because the horn stuck. With the horn blaring, I fumbled around for a fuse to shut the horn off. Failing, I drove home with it blaring. It was past eleven o'clock at night when I pulled into the driveway. My next-door neighbor ran out of his house, pulling on clothes, to see where the noise was coming from. He helped me find and cut the wire leading to the horn, silencing it forever.

The issue that night was not a time-management issue. It was a pastoral theology issue. What do pastors do with their time, and does the church understand and recognize the work that pastors do? Ultimately, I was thankful for the stuck horn and the ride home. By midnight my wife and I were laughing to the point of tears.

Congregations tend to overlook the real work of pastors when they shower their pastors with ego-boosting praise and perks. We love putting our pastors on pedestals because then we know right where we can find them. The unbiblical terms of endearment imposed on the pastor-parishioner relationship tend to make pastors beholden to their admirers. People appreciate their pastors because of the way they meet their needs, the way they're always there for them. I'm not a fan of "Pastor Appreciation Month," if the subtext says, in effect, "You work for us. You're doing a good job. Keep it up." I'm not suggesting that we shouldn't love our pastors or show them appreciation or give them gifts. But let's be clear. Pastors and people work together under Christ's lordship. The pastor is not a substitute for Christ. Pastors offer leadership to an every-member ministry team. They challenge the household of faith on a host of difficult cultural issues. It's not their job to cater to passive recipients of spiritual services.

When I was teaching full time in a seminary in Toronto, I became a part-time teaching pastor in a small, urban, ethnically diverse church. A middle-aged couple, influential in the church, asked my wife and me out for dinner on a Friday night in mid-January. I reached the end of that week exhausted and sick with the flu. If I had known the couple who invited us out better, I would have canceled our plans without a second thought, but I was afraid that I might offend them. Promptly at six o'clock in the evening, the doorbell rang. I went to answer the door, as Virginia gave last-minute instructions to the babysitter. Before I realized what was happening, a crowd shouted, "Surprise!" The door flung open, and in walked around seventy-five people into our matchbox-sized home. It was a surprise, alright—it was the very last thing that we expected or desired. Shedding winter coats and boots, the crowd was loaded with everything needed for a party: food, folding chairs, the church coffee urn, and even a huge chocolate layer cake with "Welcome to Our Church" written in white frosting.

Dear old grandmothers braved the winter weather to come and sit on church folding chairs lined up in rows in our little living room, while hyper kids ran up and down the stairs. Every conceivable space in our house was crammed with people who were ready to party. Virginia and I rushed around trying to help the "hostesses" set the food out and find needed kitchen utensils. With a pounding headache, I went upstairs to find some aspirin in the bathroom cabinet and was greeted by two teenagers sitting on metal chairs in the bathtub, eating chocolate cake. It was an unforgettable evening, but by the time they all left, at around midnight, I wasn't sure I wanted to see these people again—though they undoubtedly meant well.

Congregations need pastors to do their holy work: preaching, spiritual direction, worship leading, and prayer, but in the household of faith it was always meant to be a working partnership of shared ministry—not in theory, but for real. Everybody has holy work to do. Pastors are parables of Christ, not symbols or stand-ins for Christ. They are constantly pointing everyone to Christ. Genuine friendship is different from ingratiating favoritism. To set pastors apart for the work they do is not to set them up for living the Christian life in our place. If pastoral ministry is all about recited prayers, meeting people's felt needs, and showing them that you care, then it is, of all jobs, the most miserable. The search for vocational holiness, pastoral integrity, and true servant leadership is a daily challenge pursued over a lifetime. The traditional model of ministry has often failed to grasp a true biblical theology of ministry. Both types, the traditional pastor and the modern professional, place pastors on a pedestal and render ordinary believers passive and dependent.

## THE FLOCK

The biblical image of the shepherd and the flock has been misconstrued and misunderstood. The metaphor became twisted into something that was never intended by the New Testament. Tradition reinforced the notion that the shepherd is actively in charge and the flock is passively submissive. John Chrysostom seemed to take the imagery of the shepherd and the flock literally. Those entrusted with the care of souls must surpass all others and soar above them in excellence of spirit. "Let the difference between shepherd and sheep," he asserted, "be as great as the distinction between rational and irrational creatures, not to say even more, since matters of much greater moment are at stake."[3] He viewed the superiority of the pastor over his flock in ontological terms: the very being of the priest, through ordination, was on an altogether different plane than mere mortals. I wish that John Chrysostom had contemplated Jesus's retort to the Pharisees when he said, "How much more valuable is a person than a sheep!" (Matt. 12:12).

There is a downside to the shepherd's high calling. John held that the pastor is responsible for not only his own sins but the sins of people. Like the ancient prophet Ezekiel, John held that the pastor is responsible for speaking out and dissuading people of their evil ways (Ezek. 3:17–19). If he did not warn them, he would be held accountable for their sins and their blood would be upon him. John insisted that the pastor by virtue of his office "stands in the most utmost peril for the sins of others."[4] This is why he claimed it was much easier to live as a monk in the wilderness than as a pastor in the city. The monk had only himself to worry about, but the pastor was morally and spiritually responsible for everyone in the flock. John imposed on the priestly office a tremendous burden of conscience.

The impact of the Reformation was great, but it did not change the dynamic between the active shepherd and the passive flock. The ontological or mystical superiority of the ordained person became and remains a functional or practical superiority. The difference between the shepherd and his flock is not between a rational man and irrational creatures, but between the pastor as conscientious parent and the congregation as infant children.

Puritan pastor Richard Baxter's seventeenth-century interpretation of the shepherd and flock metaphor reinforces the model of the active pastor and the passive flock. The apostle Paul charged the elders of the church at Ephesus with the responsibility of oversight: "Keep watch over yourselves and all the flock of which the Holy Spirit has made you overseers." Baxter, on the other hand, stressed

---

3    Chrysostom, *On the Priesthood*, 54.
4    Chrysostom, *On the Priesthood*, 103.

"that every flock should have its own pastor, and every pastor its own flock." Instead of entrusting a ministry team with the task of oversight, Baxter saw a single pastor exercising oversight over a particular congregation. "From this relation of pastor and flock, arise all the duties which they mutually owe to each other."[5]

Baxter acknowledged the burden of this responsibility and advised that congregations ought to be kept small enough for pastors to fulfill their duties. "God will not lay upon us natural impossibilities: he will not bind men to leap up to the moon, to touch the stars, or to number the sands of the sea."[6] However, Baxter's proposed solution to "natural impossibilities" was not every-member ministry, the gifts of the Spirit, and the priesthood of all believers, but smaller congregations. He wrote, "If the pastoral office consists in overseeing all the flock, then surely the number of souls under the care of each pastor must not be greater than he is able to take such heed to as is here required."[7] Baxter warned that God would require the blood of so many parishes at the hands of bishops who tried to do too much.

Nor was Baxter impressed with pastors who gave themselves to preaching and let others carry out spiritual discipline for the flock. Baxter called for the pastor to know the spiritual condition of each and every person under his charge: "Does not a careful shepherd look after every individual sheep?"[8] Baxter was not against hiring ministerial assistants to share oversight responsibilities. He advised pastors to cut their salaries if it was necessary to do so. Apparently, it never occurred to him that the body was gifted by the Spirit to look after itself. Instead of every-member ministry, Baxter envisioned a single minister ministering to a flock small enough for the pastor to know everyone personally. George Hunter concludes that for the most part laypeople "are

---

5    Richard Baxter, *The Reformed Pastor*, ed. William Brown (Carlisle, PA: The Banner of Truth Trust, 2007), 88; see also Acts 20:28.
6    Baxter, *The Reformed Pastor*, 88.
7    Baxter, *The Reformed Pastor*, 88.
8    Baxter, *The Reformed Pastor*, 91.

essentially spectators," or at best, third-string players waiting for the chance opportunity to serve when the ordained minister is unable to perform his duties.[9]

For Baxter, the metaphor of the flock is an apt description of a docile, needy Christendom congregation, dependent on the pastor for virtually everything. By the time he refers to 1 Peter 2:9, he seems unaware of the implications of the priesthood of all believers. Baxter uses the description of the church as "a chosen generation, a royal priesthood, a holy nation, a peculiar people," as an incentive for pastors to be diligent in their work and to attend to these valuable yet needy people. Baxter writes, "What a high honor is it to be but one of them, yes, but a doorkeeper in the house of God! But to be the priest of these priests, and the ruler of these kings—this is such an honor as multiplies your obligations to diligence and fidelity in so noble an employment."[10]

Most pastors at some point in their ministry have had to deal with these conventional Christendom expectations. It never seems to fail—a few lay leaders see it as their responsibility to hold their pastor accountable for living up to a Baxter-style pastoral job description. They virtually excuse themselves of any ministry responsibility while taking it upon themselves to make sure that the pastor is doing all that is expected of him. Pastors often feel like failures because they cannot satisfy the excessive demands and burdens placed upon them. But, ironically, they are often rendered powerless by lay leaders who treat them as employees—who act as if the pastor works for them because they are paying the pastor's salary. Such pastors have all the traditional burdens without any of the traditional authority. An elder once told me that his sole responsibility was to make sure that I did my job. He was not an overbearing, negative person. He always encouraged me. But he saw his "job" as an elder to be "police the pastor." Obviously, I did a poor

---

9   George Hunter, *Radical Outreach: The Recovery of Apostolic Ministry and Evangelism* (Nashville: Abingdon, 2003), 105–7.

10  Baxter, *The Reformed Pastor*, 131.

job of convincing him of his pastoral responsibilities, especially as an elder, in the priesthood of all believers.

In a heated exchange with the Pharisees, Jesus described himself as the good shepherd who knows his sheep by name, and the sheep know his voice. His sheep will not follow a stranger; they only will follow him. The good shepherd leads and protects them (John 10). The good shepherd discourse is filled with messianic significance. It reveals Jesus's messianic self-understanding: "I am the gate for the sheep," and "I am the good shepherd. The good shepherd lays down his life for the sheep" (John 10:7, 11).

Thomas Oden insists, "This is no incidental, take-it-or-leave-it image for ministry. Consistently it remains the overarching analogy under which all descriptions and functions of ministry tend to be embraced: the good pastor whose vigilant caring is an expression of Christ's own eternal caring."[11] However, this hasty and unwarranted leap from Jesus's messianic witness to a pastor's role and responsibility is problematic. There is no more interpretative justification for equating Jesus, the Good Shepherd, with the pastor, than rewriting Psalm 23 to read "Pastor Jones is my Shepherd, I shall not want." All disciples can learn from Jesus's self-description of care and sacrifice and all Christians ought to model their lives after their Lord and Savior. Primarily, this is a messianic passage that shapes our understanding of Jesus and deepens our passion for Christ. Secondarily, the model of Christ provides crucial spiritual direction for all disciples, including pastors and parents. I am afraid that what the apostle John said about the Pharisees may be true for theologians who claim this passage is mainly about pastors. "Jesus used this figure of speech, but the Pharisees did not understand what he was telling them" (John 10:6).

## SHEPHERDS

The apostle Peter wrote to believers facing two challenges: living in the household of faith and living in an alien and hostile culture.

---

11   Oden, *Pastoral Theology*, 52

His pastoral letter exudes humility and models the love and respect shepherds need for God's flock. He addresses the elders only after offering spiritual direction for all believers. His primary exhortation is focused on all believers, to his "dear friends" to whom he has made his case for salvation, sanctification, solidarity, submission, and suffering. He offers a strategy for engaging a hostile culture and experiencing joy in the messianic community that is rooted in the example and empowerment of Jesus Christ. To that full picture he now brings a word of exhortation to the shepherds of God's flock, who serve under the Good Shepherd, Jesus Christ.[12]

For Peter, there is no difference between ordinary believers and elders when it comes to obedience, holiness, devotion, and sacrifice. Peter only knows one form of spiritual maturity, which he illustrates by highlighting faithful slaves and wives. He offers a bottom-up profile of the true disciple. There is no greater gift given than the gift of the "new birth into a living hope through the resurrection of Jesus Christ" and no higher status than being heir to the gracious gift of life (1 Peter 1:3; 3:7). There is no higher vow than our baptismal vow.

Peter's appeal to the elders rests on a threefold identification: their shared responsibility, their shared experience, and their shared glory. He describes himself as a co-elder, a word he may have coined to emphasize their coworking relationship.[13] Peter sees himself as a peer, not a superior; as a brother, not an official. He is one with them in the responsibility of shepherding the household of faith.

Peter begins with an imperative: *Be shepherds.* The pastoral image implies responsibility, rather than a proud position symbolizing authority. Peter's use of the metaphor invokes a rich history of biblical meaning stretching from Abraham to Jesus. Shepherds were working-class laborers who gathered, guided, and protected their flocks. Peter reiterates the God-centered nature of shepherding in three ways.

---

12  Webster, *Outposts of Hope*, 140–51.
13  John H. Elliott, *1 Peter*, The Anchor Yale Bible (New Haven, CT: Yale University Press, 2001), 817.

First, shepherds are entrusted with a flock that belongs to God, not themselves. Their work is always a matter of stewardship, not ownership. Pastors who refer to "my people" ought to be mindful that the people belong to God and God alone.

Second, the willingness of shepherds to do the work of shepherding is inspired and instructed by the will of God, not by an ambitious ego or a needy personality. The appearance of godliness is no substitute for the power of God (2 Tim. 3:5), and a reputation for zeal, apart from the will of God, is worthless (Rom. 10:2). Faith in Jesus and the faith of Jesus are inseparable. Whatever is done in the name of Jesus is to be done the Jesus way.

Third, all shepherds serve under the Good Shepherd and their reward comes when Christ appears. Once again, Peter draws out the eschatological perspective. He completes the triad of divine identification—God's flock, God's will, and God's glory—in a way that corresponds to his triad of solidarity: coworker, co-witness, and corecipient of "the glory to be revealed" (1 Peter 5:1, 4).

Peter concludes this brief exhortation to co-elders with considerable care. He qualifies the responsibility of shepherds to watch over God's flock with three requirements for motivation, set in tension against their contrary: "not because you must, but because you are willing . . . not pursuing dishonest gain, but eager to serve . . . not lording it over those entrusted to you, but being examples to the flock" (vv. 2–3).

*Not because you must, but because you are willing.* Unless there is a plurality of serving elders in the household of God and a shared understanding of the priesthood of all believers there is little hope for pastors to sustain a willing spirit. The joy of ministry will dissipate over time because of unbiblical and unreasonable expectations. Under the burden of an unrelenting job description, many pastors wonder why they no longer enjoy "watching over God's flock." Their "willingness" to serve is not in line with God's will and they feel worse than obligated: they feel trapped.

*Not pursuing dishonest gain, but eager to serve.* When elders are isolated and estranged from their true calling—biblical shep-

herding—they are more easily tempted to pursue "dishonest gain."
Money becomes a compensating calculation, offsetting the frustration pastors feel for playing along in the Jesus business. Peter's positive counterpoint to this mercenary malady is, simply, be "eager to serve."

*Not lording it over those entrusted to you, but being examples to the flock.* Peter warns his co-elders against spiritual malpractice. These three negative elements, distasteful duty, dishonest gain, and domination, coalesce to sabotage a gospel ministry and pave the way for religion as usual. Peter's concern echoes the master's perspective:

> You know that the rulers of the Gentiles lord it over them, and their high officials exercise authority over them. Not so with you. Instead, whoever wants to become great among you must be your servant, and whoever wants to be first must be your slave—just as the Son of Man did not come to be served, but to serve, and to give his life as a ransom for many. (Matt. 20:25–28)

The way to be a shepherd is to be an example to the flock: "Not bossily telling others what to do, but tenderly showing them the way" (1 Peter 5:3 MSG). Good shepherds take after the Good Shepherd who "lays down his life for the sheep" (John 10:11). Peter's advice here is consistent with what he said earlier: "To this you were called, because Christ suffered for you, leaving you an example, that you should follow in his steps" (1 Peter 2:21).

CHAPTER 7

# SHARED VISION

*We proclaim him, admonishing and teaching every-one with all wisdom that we might present everyone fully mature in Christ. To this end I strenuously contend with all the energy Christ so powerfully works in me.*

—Colossians 1:28–29 (NIV 1984)

I n a few lines the apostle Paul declared the focus of his *mission*, the purpose of his *method*, and the power of his *means*. His mission statement focused on the evangelical proclamation of the gospel, the whole counsel of God training for all believers, and the energizing empowerment of the Holy Spirit. Paul defined the end goal as well as the means to that end. His purpose was singular, his strategy, simple, and the source of his resilient energy was Christ. The apostle's personal goal was one with his *shared vision* for the church.

## MISSION STATEMENT

Mission statements became popular in the corporate world in the 1980s and 1990s. They were widely touted as a strategic management tool designed to focus a company's purpose and goals. The corporate business world inspired a merger in Christendom between religious tradition and consumer culture. Experts taught the church how to compete for souls in a market-driven culture. Some churches became the religious equivalent of big box stores, offering uplifting performances, self-help sermons, and a myriad of support groups for the admirers of Jesus. Meanwhile the traditional church hunkered down and created their own version of cultural Christianity.

Long before management guru Peter Drucker promoted corporate mission statements, Jesus defined the mission of the church in his Great Commandment to love God and our neighbor and in his Great Commission to make disciples of all peoples (Matt. 22:37; 28:19). The apostles followed the Lord's lead and gave to the emerging church a clearly defined mission and vision (Acts 2:42). They carved out a unique identity as "God's chosen people, holy and dearly loved" (Col. 3:12). They ran the race with their eyes fixed on Jesus (Heb. 12:1–2). They set apart Christ as Lord of their hearts and proclaimed the gospel with "gentleness and respect, keeping a clear conscience" (1 Peter 3:15–16). The New Testament does a wonderful job of presenting clearly and simply the mission of the household of faith without sacrificing its depth and complexity.

Leadership teams spent hours brainstorming pithy, succinct statements designed to sum up what their church was all about. We went on retreats, employed consultants, debated it from every angle, and labored over each word until it finally became more important to finish the process and get on with the work of the church. The end result was not always impressive: "Real Jesus, Real People, Real World" or "Love God, Love the World, Love One Another." These slogans may have been better for marketing and public relations than for mission and obedience. Few questioned the enthusiastic reduction of ministry to a sound bite and its dumbing-down effect on the church. Today, attention is shifting away from mission statements to marketing strategies. We feel the need to tell our brand story and craft an image with an appealing logo. We seem intent on focusing on the pedantic at the expense of the profound. We are more concerned about packaging than product. We settle for simplicity on this side of complexity rather than giving our all for the simplicity on the other side of complexity.

In a Q&A session following a talk I gave at a pastor's conference, I was asked what our church's mission statement was. The look of disappointment on the face of the pastor when I quoted Colossians 1:28–29 was telling. In an instant, I lost all credibility. It was like I had short-circuited the creative process and cheated on an exam. The pastor's reaction reminded me of a response Ray Stedman gave when asked about his ten-year plan for Peninsula Bible Church. His ready answer was, "We don't have any. We are committed to doing consistently, year after year, the principles that God has taught us from the Word, and we plan to keep on doing that until the Lord returns." Stedman's perspective remains refreshingly New Testament.

The apostle Paul's mission statement impressed our downtown church as a beautiful description of what we ought to be about. Colossians 1:28–29 emphasized our need to proclaim the gospel, to make disciples, and to give ourselves wholeheartedly to Jesus's kingdom work. The longer I reflect on these two sentences, the more impressed I am with how they sum up a pastoral theology for the household of faith. Every word in the apostle's statement is full of meaning, beginning with the first little word, "we." It is not just pastors who proclaim Christ, "we" all do. This first-person plural "we" impressed our congregation with the shared responsibility of being the priesthood of all believers. Paul's emphasis underscores a biblical theology of the call and the solidarity of the household of faith in making disciples.

## WE THE PEOPLE

We ought to take this all-inclusive "we" seriously. We have a shared responsibility for proclaiming the gospel through word and deed. The power of the apostle's "we" should not be overlooked but acknowledged and embraced. Paul's first-person plural is not a literary *we*, nor is it in reference to his small missionary team. It is a bold, all-encompassing "we" that fits well with his emphasis on "all" and "everyone" in his mission statement. Yet, it is such a little word. We are tempted to skip over it. Calvin does. What Paul says here Calvin insists "applies to his own preaching. . . . for he has it in view to adorn his apostleship, and to claim authority for his doctrine." Instead of teaching the believer's shared responsibility to proclaim the gospel, Calvin has Paul focused on himself: "God has placed me in a lofty position, as a public herald of his secret, that the whole world, without exception, may learn from me."[1]

Like so many pastors, Calvin associated "proclamation" with what the preacher does from the pulpit, but the apostle Paul didn't think this way. His "we" was not limited to apostles and preachers but encompassed all believers. A pastor-centered ministry tends to ignore the "fellowship of believers" and reinforce the twin problems of professionalization and passivity. If we even imply that ministry primarily belongs to pastors because of their training and ordination, we exclude baptized and gifted believers from their God-appointed responsibility.

Philip Jacob Spener, an influential German pastor, wrote *Pia Desideria* (Pious Desires) in 1675 "to restore to the people the Word of God which had laid hidden."[2] He took the concept of "we" seriously and encouraged a return to New Testament practices. Spener advocated the priesthood of all believers even as he maintained respect for pastors. Instead of diminishing the effectiveness of the congregationally called minister and reducing the pastor's preaching authority, Spener saw the priesthood of all believers as strengthening the minister. He wrote,

> No damage will be done to the ministry by a proper use of this priesthood. In fact, one of the principal reasons why the ministry cannot accomplish all that it ought is that it is too weak without the help of the universal priesthood. One man is incapable of doing all that is necessary for the edification of the many persons who are generally entrusted

1    John Calvin, *Commentary on Galatians and Ephesians* (Grand Rapids: Baker, 1981), 170–71.
2    Philip Jacob Spener, *Pia Desideria*, trans. Theodore G. Tappert (Philadelphia: Fortress, 1964), 92.

to his pastoral care. However, if the priests do their duty, the minister, as director and oldest brother, has splendid assistance in the performance of his duties and his public and private acts, and thus his burden will not be too heavy.[3]

Spener believed that vocational holiness belonged to all believers. All believers were gifted in the Spirit and ministers of the gospel. He claimed that disciple-making responsibilities belonged to all believers.[4] Spener claimed that the difference between a pastor and a faithful brother and sister in Christ is a difference in gifts and designated responsibilities. Instead of a power struggle between them, there ought to be a positive tension, where "iron sharpens iron," and each makes the other better and stronger than they would be without the other.

Pastors can take the lead in overcoming believer passivity and encourage full participation in gospel ministry. All believers deserve the respect and support of the pastoral team in living out their commitment to Christ. By emphasizing a theology of the call and the priesthood of all believers, pastors expand the disciples understanding of personal salvation to include the gospel impact on all of life. Pastoral teaching on faith and vocation, the Sermon on the Mount, the gifts of the Spirit, and praying the Psalms, offers the household of faith the necessary wisdom to engage the world with the gospel.

Pastors can show genuine interest in the working lives of their fellow believers. They may encourage job-related prayer requests. They may make an appointment and visit believers at their work site. They may lead specially designed Bible studies for nurses and doctors, public school teachers, and businesspeople. Over several years I participated with a group of coaches, educators, athletic directors, kinesiologists, and theologians to develop a Christian perspective on sports. The benefit for me as a pastor was great, because being in the company of these brothers and sisters in Christ gave me a perspective on ministering to families immersed in sports and athletics.

---

3    Spener, *Pia Desideria*, 95.
4    Spener, *Pia Desideria*, 94.

Churches can pray for their public and private school teachers in the congregation and set them apart for the work of the Lord. After I read Chap Clark's *Hurt: Inside the World of Today's Teenagers,* I ordered ten copies for each of our high school teachers.[5] I suggested that we read it together and then gather at my home for dinner and a discussion. It was a great evening, and in their company I became aware of the pressures and opportunities that our *missionary* teachers were facing. We ended the evening praying for one another.

There are any number of professions represented in our churches that would benefit from gathering together for serious Bible study and discussion on the impact of Christ on their professions. It is worth exploring together what it means to be a devoted follower of Jesus Christ in banking or real estate or construction or policing. Personally, and pastorally, I've only scratched the surface on the kind of faith and vocation work that needs to be done.

There are some thirty different words used for communicating the gospel in the New Testament. These include *proclaim, announce, preach, teach, explain, speak, say, testify, persuade, confess, charge,* and *admonish.* Theologian Hans Küng concludes, "The variety of different kinds of preaching allows each and every one to make his [or her] contribution towards the preaching of the message. . . . All are called to preach the Gospel in the sense of their personal Christian witness, without being all called to preach in a narrow sense of the word or to be theologians."[6]

A pastoral theology for the household of faith inherently respects all believers and honors the priesthood of all believers. We need not ignore the missionaries in our midst. When my uncle Paul died, we traveled to Wisconsin for his funeral. Paul lived into his eighties and was well-known throughout his career in publishing and then into retirement as a committed follower of Christ. He was gifted in relating to all types of people, especially young people. He

---

5    Chap Clark, *Hurt: Inside the World of Today's Teenagers* (Grand Rapids: Baker, 2004).
6    Hans Küng, *The Church* (Garden City, NY: Doubleday, 1976), 479, 481.

showed real love and friendship and demonstrated genuine interest and concern for others. He had a way of showing compassion and sharing Christ with people that was well received because it was authentic. His memorial service was packed with young people whom he befriended and loved in Christ. Several of his grand-children spoke. They eulogized their grandfather and gave credit to the power of the gospel in his life. They thanked the Lord for uncle Paul's wisdom, friendship, and love, and as they shared their remembrances you could hear the proverbial pin drop.

Then the senior pastor came to the pulpit and, with an air of self-importance, announced that it was now his responsibility to preach the gospel. Even though several young people had testified to the power of the gospel in Paul's life, he acted as if only his sermon counted. His text was Luke 15, the parable of the prodigal son. He began his sermon by stressing my uncle's lostness, saying, "We all know that at some point Paul was lost. He had to be lost, so he must have been like the prodigal son." Ironically, the only person in the story the pastor could identify with was the wayward lost son. It never occurred to him that uncle Paul's gospel-shaped life was a beautiful example of the Father's love. Instead of exploring how the gospel shaped my uncle's life and witness, the pastor came across like the nose-out-of-joint elder brother who went through life dutifully doing his job and feeling resentful. Perhaps the pastor's reticence stemmed from his inability to see that this lay leader was a trusted guide to many—a true proclaimer of Christ, who embodied the Father's love.

## PROCLAIMING TRUTH

One of the oldest missions in California, San Diego de Alcala Mission, is surrounded by lush vegetation, beautiful flowers, and tall trees. It is a garden, but it used to be a desert. Pictures in the museum dating back to the 1800s reveal a barren brown hillside, a stark landscape, nothing but scrub brush, dirt, and rocks. There are no gardens in San Diego that were not planted, watered, pro-tected, and cared for. The trees that are indigenous to this part of the country belong in a desert because that is what San Diego would be if it were not for constant irrigation. What is true for botanical growth in San Diego is also true for spiritual growth in the household of faith. Growing in Christ does not happen automatically. Spiritual growth is the work of the Holy Spirit in believers who desire to grow in the grace and knowledge of the Lord Jesus Christ.

The apostle Paul uses three verbs in the present tense to stress the continuing practice of the church to proclaim Christ. All three verbs go together to describe the delivery of the gospel. To *proclaim* is to communicate the gospel in a compelling way. Proclamation implies an intensity and seriousness not found in routine communication. Proclamation is not sermonic, decorative, homiletical speech. It doesn't sound like a radio broadcast or a television preacher. It sounds like Jesus. It is life-on-life, person-to-person communication in community that addresses the mind and the heart. Proclamation refuses the language of the marketplace. It is not pitching a product to consumers. Proclamation rejects political language. It is not trying to win voters. Proclamation, Peterson writes, "grabs for the jugular. . . . It is intestinal. It is root language."[7]

Writer Tim Stafford describes an object lesson that Pastor Stephen Bilynskyj uses with new members. He starts with a jar full of beans and he asks them to guess how many beans are in the jar. On a big pad of paper, he writes down their estimates. Then, next to the estimates, he helps them make another list: their favorite songs. When the lists are complete, he reveals the actual number of beans in the jar. The whole class looks over the guesses, to see which estimate was closest to being right. Bilynskyj then turns to the list of favorite songs. "And which one of these is closest to being right?" he asks. The students protest that there is no "right answer"; a person's favorite song is purely a matter of taste. Bilynskyj, who holds a PhD

---

7    Eugene H. Peterson, *Answering God: The Psalms as Tools for Prayer* (San Francisco: Harper and Row, 1989), 11.

in philosophy from Notre Dame, says, "When you decide what to believe in terms of your faith, is that more like guessing the number of beans, or more like choosing your favorite song?"

Always, Bilynskyj says, from old as well as young, he gets the same answer: choosing one's faith is more like choosing a favorite song. He then proceeds to argue them out of it, because faith in Christ is not a question of taste, but a matter of fact. "Favorite-song theology" leaves the impression that everyone has a right to their opinion when it comes to faith in Christ. There is no right or wrong, there is no true or false, because it is a matter of taste.[8]

Francis Schaeffer came to Wheaton College in the 1960s to give a series of lectures based on the prophet Jeremiah; these addresses were later published in a book entitled *Death in the City*. At the time, America was in the throes of the sexual revolution, race riots, and anti-war demonstrations. College campuses were in turmoil. Society was shaken. Conventional wisdom was crumbling. Schaeffer wore his hair long and dressed in hiking knickers. He looked like he had just come down from the Swiss Alps, because he had. He and his wife Edith cofounded a community in Switzerland called L'Abri to reach out to young people searching for meaning and significance. Francis Schaeffer had the voice and manner of a prophet and, like Jeremiah, there was a fire in his bones. He insisted on the reality of true "Truth." Truth with a capital "T." Schaeffer proclaimed, "God is there, and he is not silent."[9] To make his point, Schaeffer wore a doctor's white lab coat to symbolize that truth is not limited to the empirical sciences. All truth is God's truth. Christians, he argued, follow a countercultural path to wisdom.

Sociologist Robert Wuthnow calls today's twenty- and thirty-year-olds a generation of tinkerers. They put life together "by

---

8   Tim Stafford, "'Favorite-Song' Theology," *Christianity Today*, September 14, 1992, 36–38.

9   Francis Schaeffer, introduction to *He Is There and He Is Not Silent* (Carol Stream, IL: Tyndale, 2001).

improvising, by piecing together an idea from here, a skill from there, and a contact from somewhere else." They have a "do-it-yourself" mentality, as they cobble together a customized lifestyle.[10] However, Christ's followers are not their own best authority. They are not in charge of piecing together a customized worldview that works for them in a pluralistic culture. Francis Schaeffer claimed that by embracing the wisdom of God revealed in Jesus, Christians countered the ways of acquiring knowledge in the culture. Instead of rummaging through the junkyard of pop culture or relying on the traditions and trends of the academy, the believer seeks God with her whole being. Like the psalmist, she articulates God's laws, rejoices in the Lord's statutes, meditates on his precepts, and delights in his decrees. She lets the word of Christ dwell in her richly as she teaches and admonishes herself and others with all wisdom (Col. 3:16). Our heavenly Father answers the prayer of his Son on our behalf, "Sanctify them by the truth; your word is truth" (John 17:17).

A friend of mine spent twenty years listening to sermons and attending Sunday school classes before taking the Bible seriously. Ray admits that the Bible had virtually no impact on his business career. He saw it as a religious book filled with idealistic platitudes and pious sayings. He respected its aura of sacred importance but found it hopelessly impractical for succeeding in the workplace. Only after a serious car accident and some deep soul-searching did he wake up to the practical significance of the Bible for daily living. Slowly, Ray began to study and internalize the Word of God. He began to take the Bible seriously.

In obedience to the Word, he began changing the way he did business. His priorities and values were transformed. His family became more important to him than his career. He altered his old habit of slanting the truth to make himself and his department look better. For years he had been able to sell customers more technology

---

10   Robert Wuthnow, *After the Baby Boomers: How Twenty-and-Thirty-Somethings Are Shaping the Future of American Religion* (Princeton, NJ: Princeton University Press, 2007), 14.

than they needed, thinking that if they were foolish enough to fall for his sales pitch, too bad for them. Now, Ray could no longer do that. He found himself persuading customers to buy less rather than more, depending on their need. The symbols of status became less important. He tried to befriend people in the company whom he had previously disliked. He sought to rectify injustices that in the past he would have ignored or condoned. In short, he began living for the kingdom of God instead of the corporation. The mix of secular values and religious piety that had existed for so many years was no longer possible.

My friend's past was like that of the person described by James who, after looking at himself in the mirror, immediately forgot what he looked like. His understanding of the Bible never penetrated his self-absorbed little world of ambition and success strategies. Biblical truth went in one ear and out the other. He deceived himself in thinking that he was a fine, upstanding Christian. He almost had to die before he took the truth of Christ seriously. One of the highlights of my teaching ministry was when Ray and I co-taught a course on Christians in business. To our surprise we had more than sixty students take the course, including forty-four businesspeople.

## EXPLANATION

Proclamation implies confidence and conviction. We are not meant to be shy or timid about proclaiming Christ. Men and women commend the truth of Christ with a holy boldness. As Jesus said, "If you hold to my teaching, you are really my disciples. Then you will know the truth, and the truth will set you free" (John 8:31–32). Paul declared, "I am not ashamed of the gospel, because it is the power of God that brings salvation to everyone who believes: first to the Jew, then to the Gentile. For in the gospel the righteousness of God is revealed, a righteousness that is by faith from first to last, just as it is written: 'The righteous will live by faith'" (Rom. 1:16–17). Luther, in his response to Erasmus, reminds us of the importance of an unambiguous assertion of gospel truth:

To take no pleasure in assertions is not the mark of a Christian heart; indeed, one must delight in assertions to be a Christian at all. . . . By "assertion" I mean staunchly holding your ground, stating your position, confessing it, defending it and persevering in it unvanquished. . . . And I am talking about the assertion of what has been delivered to us from above in the Sacred Scriptures. . . . Take away assertions, and you take away Christianity. Why, the Holy Spirit is given to Christians from heaven in order that He may glorify Christ and in them confess Him even unto death—and is this not assertion, to die for what you confess and assert?[11]

This proclamation does not need a pulpit. On the road to Emmaus, Jesus met up with two heartbroken disciples. They didn't recognize Jesus and mistook him for a stranger. They spoke of Jesus in the past tense: "He *was* a prophet, powerful in word and deed before God and all the people" (Luke 24:19, emphasis mine). They were unaware that they were airing their despair and confusion to the risen Lord himself. It was then that Jesus pivoted the conversation, saying, "How foolish you are, and how slow to believe all that the prophets have spoken! Did not the Messiah have to suffer these things and then enter his glory?" (Luke 24:25–26). Jesus challenged them on an intellectual level. He made "thinking," not "feeling," the issue. His no-nonsense, impatient tone confronted these two disciples with the truth. It was as if he asked, "What were you thinking? Have you read your Bibles?" Jesus insisted on the importance of the mind. He lifted the discussion out of the realm of the subjective self and placed it in the context of objective truth.

The way in which Jesus sought to penetrate their confusion and bring clarity is significant. He used content—revelational content. He appealed to their cognitive grasp of revelation. The current epis-

---

11  Martin Luther, *The Bondage of the Will,* trans. J. I. Packer and O. R. Johnston (Old Tappan, NJ: Fleming H. Revell, 1990), 66–67.

temological bias against *thinking* distances people from the truth. Jesus told the story of salvation history: "And beginning with Moses and all the Prophets, he *explained* to them what was said in all the Scriptures concerning himself" (Luke 24:27). I wish we had Jesus's conversation verbatim, but even if we did, it wouldn't add anything to what we already know from the Word of God. However, what a wonderful experience it must have been for these two disciples to hear Jesus explain "all the Scriptures concerning himself." I imagine Jesus included Abel's sacrificial lamb, Abraham at the altar with Isaac, Job's cry ("I know that my Redeemer lives and that in the end he will stand on the earth and after my skin has been destroyed yet in my flesh I will see him"; Job 19:25–26), Israel's Passover lamb, Moses raising the serpent in the wilderness, David's prayer ("My God, my God, why have you forsaken me?"; Ps. 22:1), Isaiah's picture of the suffering servant, Daniel's vision of the victorious Son of Man, and Zechariah's humble king, his unappreciated shepherd. "And beginning with Moses and all the Prophets" implies that the whole account was given, from Genesis to Malachi.

There is an undeserved mystique that surrounds the Bible that keeps even earnest believers from grasping its meaning. We make the text out to be unwieldy and complicated. On the one hand, we have parsed, translated, exegeted, researched, debated, and interpreted the text—to the point of abstraction and learned sophistry. And, on the other, we have reduced the text to sound bites, PowerPoint outlines, and anecdotal illustrations. Bad sermons give the impression that the Bible is a moralistic storybook or a self-help guidebook or a resource for motivational speakers. Poor scholarship gives the impression that the Bible is undependable, fraught with wild and strange variants, and competing, contradictory ideas. Many churchgoing readers see the Bible as a huge undifferentiated mass of spiritual material designed to inspire devotional thoughts, or they see it as "the good book" with secrets for success and stories of courage. Jesus shared the thrust of salvation history and its climax in seven miles. Jesus surveyed the biblical narrative in the time it took to walk to Emmaus. He drew out its salvation-making, history-changing, life-transforming significance. The two disciples felt the impact of the word of God rightly divided: "Were not our hearts burning within us while he talked with us on the road and opened the Scriptures to us?" (Luke 24: 32). Has this ever happened to you? You feel your adrenaline surge as your pulse quickens at the impact of God's truth.

CHAPTER 8

# PASTOR-THEOLOGIAN

*Theology serves the church by helping shape its collective imagination so that its image of its body life, and everything else, is governed by the gospel message at the heart of the master story that unifies Scripture: what God was doing by anticipation in Israel, and ultimately in Christ, to provide light to the nations, reconcile all things to himself, and renew creation.*[1]

—Kevin Vanhoozer

If pastoring consists in pastors proving that they care, then we've missed the meaning of pastoral ministry.[2] The old saying, "People don't care how much you know, until they know how much you care" sounds great to people who feel entitled to a pastor's attention, but when pastor's understand their calling in this way laypersons are given an excuse to neglect their own personal response to the Word of God. The saying reiterates the "one-way" mindset of ministry referenced earlier and supports the clergy/laity divide. It also enables a needy congregation. Pastors should

---

1  See Keven J. Vanhoozer, *Hearers and Doers: A Pastor's Guide to Making Disciples through Scripture and Doctrine* (Bellingham, WA: Lexham, 2019), 10.
2  McKnight, *Pastor Paul*, 192.

be all for caring and showing love, but they are not called to placate passive recipients of religious services. Cut-flower prayers are
Christendom's bread and butter, to the neglect of "justice, mercy
and faithfulness" (Matt. 23:23). Catering to felt needs as a prerequisite for pastoral ministry is a poor substitute for growing in the
grace and knowledge of the Lord Jesus Christ. William Willimon
puts it this way:

> One of the great challenges of contemporary pastoral
> ministry is having something more important to do in
> our ministry than simply offering love and service to
> people. Too few pastors rise above simple congregational
> maintenance, have no higher goal in their ministry than
> mushy, ill-defined "love" or "presence." To find ourselves
> yoked, bound to our profession of faith, namely that
> Christ really is present in Word and Sacrament, over-
> turning the world through us—this is great grace.[3]

Congregations need to be better informed on the nature and
purpose of pastoral ministry, and pastors need to serve their
congregations as biblical theologians with prophetic and pastoral
insight. Instead of being a club for the admirers of Jesus, we are a
company of the followers of the crucified and risen Messiah. Our
task is making disciples.

Stanley Hauerwas described this difference as between a church
that exists to make people feel good and a church that exists as
an "outpost of hope" in a fallen and needy world. It is the difference between cheap and costly grace. It is the difference between
market-driven consumers and resident aliens whose identity is in
Christ. It is the difference between passive recipients of spiritual
services and disciples who offer themselves as living sacrifices
(Rom. 12:1).

---

3    Willimon, *Pastor*, 22.

The church seems caught in an irresolvable tension today. Insofar as we are able to maintain any presence in
modern society, we do so by being communities of care.
Pastors become primarily people who care. Any attempt
in such a context for the church to be a disciplined
and discipling community seems antithetical to being
a community of care. As a result, the care the church
gives, while often quite impressive and compassionate,
lacks the rationale to build the church as a community
capable of standing against the powers we confront.[4]

Meeting the needs of the body of Christ is important, but this is the
shared responsibility of the fellowship of believers. Need-meeting
alone is not the business of the church. Disciple-making is. Pastors
may be gifted relationally; to an extent, they must be. Loving people with the love of Christ is a prerequisite for pastoral ministry.
Pastors make home visits, lunch appointments, phone calls, and
hospital visits, because they want to. They love interacting with all
sorts of people, because its their calling. Relating to the body of
Christ is a top priority, but pastoring also involves proclaiming the
gospel, leading in worship, helping people to grow in their faith,
and guiding them in a costly discipleship. Real encounters are
part of every faithful and fruitful pastor's life, but the burden and
blessing of a relational ministry must be spread among brothers
and sisters in Christ in the household of faith. Otherwise, pastors,
understandably, will grow tired of having to prove themselves
relationally over and over again to passive recipients of spiritual
services. Pastors are theologians, primarily, not therapists. Their
primary aim is not to make people feel good about themselves,
but to guide them by the whole counsel of God.

---

4    Stanley Hauerwas, *After Christendom? How the Church Is to Behave if Free-
     dom, Justice, and a Christian Nation Are Bad Ideas* (Nashville: Abingdon,
     1991), 93.

## FELLOWSHIP OF BELIEVERS

The apostle Paul's description of the household of faith in Colossians revolutionizes our understanding of the fellowship of believers. In Christ, we have been given a new identity. By God's grace we are a "chosen people, holy and dearly loved" (Col. 3:12). We are no longer defined by our broken past or our religious self-righteousness or our dysfunctional families. Once we were alienated from God and enemies to our own minds, but now we have been reconciled to God because of the atoning sacrifice of Christ (Col. 1:21–23). We have been reborn into a living hope (1 Peter 1:3).

At a dinner party, I was seated across from the host's mother, who had recently started attending our church. "There's something I must share with you," she began. "My son convinced me to come to church. He said that if I came to church for six weeks, he would never bug me about going to church again." I said to her that I had heard of parents saying that to their young-adult children, but never the other way around. She continued, "I have been away from the church for fifteen years. I haven't felt comfortable in church ever since my husband left me. Whenever I tried to go back to church, I felt so angry and hurt that I could not bring myself to go." She relayed that the first Sunday she attended was a Sunday I preached from the prophet Jeremiah. The theme of my sermon was "God, the jilted lover." She said, "Suddenly, I realized that what my husband did to me, I did to God. The thought of it overwhelmed me. I rejected God's love for all of these years because my husband had left me. God hadn't rejected me. I had rejected God. I turned my back on God."

Paul admonishes the chosen, holy, and dearly loved people of God to clothe themselves with "compassion, kindness, humility, gentleness and patience" (Col. 3:12). Each and every believer takes off the clothing of the old self (i.e., sexual immorality, impurity, lust, evil desires, greed, anger, rage, malice, slander, and abusive language) and puts on the former clothing, which is the clothing of the new self. Instead of a religious official modeling "Christian" virtue, we have a fellowship of believers, clothed in righteousness, gifted in the Spirit, putting on love, "which binds [all the virtues] together in perfect unity" (Col. 3:14). The body of Christ is alive in the Spirit, a living, breathing organism, which cannot long endure on organizational genius and institutional endowments. This is why Paul admonishes the whole church to "let the peace of Christ rule in your hearts" and "let the word of Christ dwell in you richly as you teach and admonish one another with all wisdom" (Col. 3:15–16). We are in this together, and whatever we do, "whether in word or deed," we do it "in the name of the Lord Jesus, giving thanks to God the Father through him" (Col. 3:17).

## DISCIPLE-MAKING

Paul's mission statement emphasizes the disciple-making art of the household of faith. His verbal strategy—to proclaim, admonish, and teach—covers the pedagogical scope of the priesthood of all believers and suggests the full range of spiritual direction. The active witness of the whole church is in service of the "God-breathed" Scripture, which is "useful for teaching, rebuking, correcting and training in righteousness, so that the servant of God may be thoroughly equipped for every good work" (2 Tim. 3:16–17). We have no other message than the truth revealed in God's Word, the Bible. Our method of making disciples is to preach "Jesus Christ and him crucified" (1 Cor. 2:2). Every aspect of God's mission for the church is rooted in the Word of God; every evangelistic and humanitarian effort verbalizes and materializes the gospel. Artist Makoto Fujimura reminds us that there "is a huge gap between informational knowing and the actual knowing of making." He continues, quoting philosopher Esther Meek, "If knowing is care at its core, caring leads to knowing. To know is to love; to love will be to know."[5] This is just as the apostle Paul prayed, that our love would "abound more and

---

5    Makoto Fujimura, *Art and Truth: A Theology of Making* (New Haven, CT: Yale University Press, 2020), 61.

more in knowledge and depth of insight, so that [we] may be able to discern what is best and may be pure and blameless for the day of Christ, filled with the fruit of righteousness that comes through Jesus Christ—to the glory and praise of God" (Phil. 1:9–11).

To the believers in Corinth, the apostle Paul expressed his mission this way: "For I resolved to know nothing while I was with you except Jesus Christ and him crucified" (1 Cor. 2:2). This basic, bedrock truth explains what Paul meant when he said, "For no one can lay any foundation other than the one already laid, which is Jesus Christ" (1 Cor. 3:11). Some have felt that Paul's resolve to know nothing but Christ crucified in Corinth was in reaction to his attempt to explain the gospel to Athenian intellectuals. Instead of debating and dialoguing as he did in Athens, he gave a simple plan of salvation to the Corinthians. However, we have no evidence for this reductionistic conclusion. On the contrary, Paul saw the relevance of the cross of Christ in every conceivable sphere of the believer's life.

I missed this important truth in Paul's letter until I experienced one of the best theological conferences I have ever attended. We met in a village outside of Mexico City with fifteen Latin American pastor-theologians and fifteen North American pastor-theologians. We spent three days talking theology; eating simple food; praying for the world, especially the poor; singing hymns; and sleeping on cots. One evening, one theologian delivered a talk that traced the meaning of the cross in Paul's letter to Corinth. He drew attention to the way Paul planted the cross at the center of every issue confronting the church.

For Paul, the cross of Jesus is the basis for unity in the body of Christ. To those who were ready to divide up according to their favored leader, Paul asked, "Is Christ divided? Was Paul crucified for you? Were you baptized in the name of Paul?" (1 Cor. 1:13). To those who were proud of their tolerance of sexual immorality in the church, Paul called for immediate church discipline because "Christ, our Passover lamb, has been sacrificed" (1 Cor. 5:7). He commanded Christians, "Flee from sexual immorality" because of the cross. "You are not your own; you were bought at a price. Therefore honor God with your body" (1 Cor. 6:18–20). He counseled believers to experience their freedom in Christ, regardless of their social circumstances, because of the cross. "You were bought at a price; do not become slaves of human beings" (1 Cor. 7:23). He advised refraining from eating meat that had been offered to idols if it would cause a new believer to stumble. Or else "this weak brother or sister, for whom Christ died, is destroyed by your knowledge" (1 Cor. 8:11).

Paul centered the worship life of the church in the cross. "Is not the cup of thanksgiving for which we give thanks a participation in the blood of Christ? And is not the bread that we break a participation in the body of Christ?" (1 Cor. 10:16). He warned believers against using their social positions and income to humiliate other believers. "For those who eat and drink without discerning the body of Christ eat and drink judgment on themselves" (1 Cor. 11:29). To those who questioned the reality of the bodily resurrection, Paul affirmed that the saving work of Christ on the cross depended upon the risen Lord Jesus. "For what I received I passed on to you as of first importance: that Christ died for our sins according to the Scriptures, that he was buried, that he was raised on the third day according to the Scriptures, and that he appeared to Cephas, and then to the Twelve" (1 Cor. 15:3–5). In the midst of every problem, every issue, every conflict impacting the church at Corinth, Paul brought the believers back to the finished work of Christ on the cross. Paul subsumed everything under the cross, even death itself. "The sting of death is sin, and the power of sin is the law. But thanks be to God! He gives us the victory through our Lord Jesus Christ" (1 Cor. 15:56–57). The apostle Paul was resolved to make the crucified and risen Messiah the sum and substance of his proclamation, admonition, and teaching.

## THE WORD VS. "IT'S JUST WORDS"

"It is no good asking for simple religion," wrote C. S. Lewis. "After all, real things are not simple." Lewis opposed a watered-down

Christianity that "simply says there is a good God in Heaven and everything is all right—leaving out all the difficult and terrible doctrines about sin and hell and the devil, and the redemption."[6] Even the devil knows, Lewis wrote in *The Screwtape Letters*, that "once you have made the World an end, and faith a means, you have almost won" and "it makes very little difference what kind of worldly end" is being pursued.[7]

One wonders if we have suffered some kind of incalculable loss when it comes to proclamation, admonition, and teaching. Has the communication of God's Word envisioned by the apostle become diminished in our day? Instead of heralding the gospel, are we mumbling? Instead of warning of judgment, are we making excuses? Instead of teaching, are we just trying to keep people's attention? Have the teaching gifts lost their potency, their apostolic authority, their prophetic edge, their evangelistic fervor, and their pastoral insight (Eph. 4:11)?

Our trained incapacity to think deeply about virtually anything has decidedly had an impact on preaching. Today's sermonizing takes this into account, whether intentionally or unintentionally, and seeks to compensate by trying to keep people interested through humor, anecdotes, and bullet points. It is ironic that as our culture has become more sophisticated in its methods of communication it has insisted on a simplified message. Our impatience with the message has increased as the speed of communications has increased. But it is here that we have to insist on comprehending the whole counsel of God. I believe there are many people who long for a passionate, in-depth proclamation of God's story from Genesis to Revelation.

I was in a debate with a mission director over whether to keep or remove the mission statement of faith from their website. The statement articulated the basic biblical convictions that had guided

---

6    C. S. Lewis, *Mere Christianity* (New York: HarperCollins, 2001), 40.
7    C. S. Lewis, *The Screwtape Letters with Screwtape Proposes a Toast* (New York: Macmillan, 1961), 35.

the mission for years. The director affirmed the statement but insisted on its removal because he was concerned that it might turn off potential donors, as well as the non-Christian doctors and nurses who served on our medical teams. I argued that it was an essential definition of the organization's gospel mission and that supporters and participants had a right to know what we believed. The mission director argued that if anyone was interested in our beliefs they could ask, and we would give them the mission's statement of faith. The board voted in favor of removing the statement of faith from the website. The mission director's closing argument still echoes in my mind: "It's just words."

A young ordinand stood before an assembly of Presbyterian pastors and elders to confess his faith in Christ. After he gave his testimony and statement of faith he was examined on his doctrinal convictions. He humbly articulated his belief in the reality Jesus's incarnation and in the atoning sacrifice of Christ. But the moment he finished, a veteran pastor of the presbytery rose to object. In the presence of more than a hundred clergy and lay leaders, he called these Christian doctrines barbaric and primitive. He claimed they were hopelessly out of date. He was blunt in his heresy, and he attacked the young man for his "naivete." Many were shocked at the pastor's brazen affront to Christian conviction.

In the weeks to follow, the presbytery called for a judicial commission to examine the pastor who openly dismissed the doctrine of Christ's atoning sacrifice as heretical. I was asked to serve on the commission. His unmasked disdain for biblical truth was a direct challenge to the confession of the church. Yet after multiple meetings and much debate, he was exonerated by the judicial commission with only one dissenting vote, my own. At that point, I doubted whether it would be possible for anyone to be charged with heresy in our presbytery—unless it was for his or her orthodox convictions.

I attended a one-day conference for pastors with the expectation of being challenged and spiritually fed. I asked a pastor friend to go with me. Three hours of in-depth Bible teaching on our holy vocation and a good conversation over lunch was just what my soul needed. It only took fifteen minutes to realize that my expectations for the day were sadly mistaken. Along with several hundred pastors, we were instructed pedantically in a proof text of the meanings of "deacon" and "elder." Reference was made to how many times "baptism" was used in Acts along with other miscellaneous data points. I was confused. The speaker seemed to have geared his presentation for a new-members class, and even then, it seemed like he was dumbing down the gospel. But what amazed me more was the response. A room full of seminary-trained pastors were lapping it up. They were laughing at the speaker's jokes and dutifully taking down notes. They seemed perfectly content with the banality of it all, loving every minute of it, while I was thinking that a steady diet of this kind of dribble will kill the church.

There is a growing inability of Christians to talk about their faith in Christ in any kind of meaningful way. Sermons have largely become a recital of evangelical platitudes, privately prepared, without interaction with the thinking and praying community. They are publicly performed without lasting impact, usually in a style that does not flow from or serve the text. And these days it seems that most Christians are hearing sermons designed for seekers or new Christians. The preacher is complimented for execution, not for making disciples. Thousands gather every Sunday to hear what they have heard many times before. There is a large and appreciative market of religious consumers who want to be given a recital of familiar truths. The impact of this kind of preaching is bigger auditoriums, filled with strangers who rarely fellowship beyond their familiar cliques. Consequently, it is becoming more difficult to distinguish between that which is done for spiritual growth and that which is done for public relations.[8]

Christian communication has virtually no context outside of the pulpit. No one wants to hear from the pastor about these things

---

8    Douglas D. Webster, *Text Messaging: A Conversation on Preaching* (Toronto: Clements, 2010), 11.

over lunch or in casual conversation, and most pastors only want to talk about administrative matters, church politics, visionary programs, and new trends. Any attempt to bring Jesus up in any kind of meaningful way outside the prescribed bounds feels like a violation of social etiquette. Gossip and small talk have largely replaced the gospel in every arena but the pulpit, and even there the danger now exists for the sermon to be co-opted by mere sentiment and self-expression.

We talk freely about sports, food, fashions, stocks, celebrities, and politics, but serious talk about the kingdom of God is almost nonexistent. We should not be surprised. Vast numbers of believers attend church in anonymity. One can go to church without ever uttering a word or making meaningful eye contact. An awkward greeting time will not free us up to talk about following Jesus. On religious matters many are well schooled, but they show little sign of a meaningful relationship with God. They look bored in Sunday school and find it difficult to interact with a pedantic lesson that they have heard hundreds of times before. We have little capacity for meaningful dialogue on the very truths that we say we are so committed to on Sunday. We have unwittingly retreated from the Word without noting its absence.

## TEACHING

The household of faith prioritizes Bible teaching. The seventeenth-century Puritan pastor, Richard Baxter, called for spiritual renewal and authenticity in the church. He proposed a simple method to accomplish this: teach people the fundamentals of Christian character and faith through personal tutorials and examinations. He concluded that many churchgoers were either unable or unwilling to grasp the truth of the gospel through public preaching:

> Let them that have taken most pains in public, examine their people, and try whether many of them are not nearly as ignorant and careless as if they had never heard

the gospel. For my part, I study to speak as plainly and as movingly as I can . . . and yet I frequently meet with those that have been my hearers eight or ten years, who know not whether Christ be God or man, and wonder when I tell them the history of his birth and life and death as if they had never heard it before. . . . I have found by experience, that some ignorant persons, who have been so long unprofitable hearers, have got more knowledge and remorse in half an hour's close discourse, than they did from ten years of public preaching.[9]

Baxter admitted there was nothing new or complex about this strategy. His plan for renewal was basic: "I wonder at myself," he wrote. "Why was I so long held back from doing so obvious and vital a duty?" He admonished pastors, "Make it your great and serious business to teach the fundamentals of the faith to all the members of your congregation by these private tutorials."[10] Baxter was not interested in a doctrinaire faith but in a living, applied faith, which took seriously the whole counsel of God. He advocated a disciplined faith, the opposite of a laid-back, easygoing, paint-by-number contemporary Christianity. His holistic, integrated approach knew no division between evangelism and discipleship. Outreach and edification went hand in hand. He wanted his people to learn their theology by heart, internalize Christian conviction, and actualize Christian practice.

## THE IMPOSSIBLE JOB

Ironically, pastoral theologies have a way of separating the nature and purpose of pastoral ministry from the practical context of

---

9   Richard Baxter, *The Reformed Pastor*, ed. William Brown (Carlisle, PA: The Banner of Truth Trust, 2007), 196; see J. I. Packer, *Quest for Godliness: The Puritan Vision of the Christian Life* (Wheaton, IL: Crossway, 1990), 307.
10  Richard Baxter, *The Reformed Pastor* (Portland, OR: Multnomah, 1982), 5–7.

congregational identity—that is, the household of faith, the work of disciple-making, the priesthood of all believers, the gifts of the Spirit, and God's mission for the church. The gravitational pull of institutional maintenance and success is too much for a pastoral identity rooted in the New Testament. Instead of *unlearning* the processes that cater to the religious consumer and the organization, pastors are taught that everything related to ministry depends on them. In *A Pastoral Rule for Today*, the authors only confirm that pastoral overwork, identity confusion, and personal isolation are real problems: "Demands on your time and energy include regular visitation and successful stewardship programs, membership growth and an efficient committee structure, presbytery [denominational] service and good sermons, community outreach and an attractive church school program—the list is endless." Their description of unreasonable expectations continues: "You are expected to be preacher, teacher, therapist, administrator, personnel director, organizational manager, entrepreneur, and CEO—all at the same time." These demands inevitably provoke the question, "Of all that I expected to do and be, what is worth doing and what is the core of my vocation?" Christendom expectations leave pastors feeling alone and abandoned: "Pastoral isolation intensifies uncertainty about what really matters. While most pastors are constantly in touch with people, opportunities for deep fellowship among pastors are rare. . . . Pastoral loneliness contributes to the personal and ecclesial disasters of sexual misconduct, alcohol abuse, and financial impropriety."[11]

Each time this litany of pastoral overwork, identity confusion, and personal isolation is expressed, it exposes the false premise on which today's pastoral ministry rests. Unwittingly, the collective and compounded effect of religious tradition, cultural expectation, and vocational pride have created an impossible position that lacks justification in the New Testament. It owes its existence to the legacy

---

11  John P. Burgess, Jerry Andrews, and Joseph D. Small, *A Pastoral Rule for Today* (Downers Grove, IL: InterVarsity Press, 2019), 164–65.

of the medieval church's sacerdotal priesthood and Christendom. It generates either guilt and insecurity or pride and ambition in all who attempt to assume it. This is why we insist that the unlearning curve is essential if we expect pastors to be pastors and enjoy serving Christ.

A biblical pastoral theology needs to go back to the New Testament's understanding of the household of faith and explore the significance of discipleship—the gifts of the Spirit, every-member ministry, and a plurality of spiritual leaders. When these elements fail to shape the church, we are left with a titular head of a human organization who offers spiritual services to passive recipients of religion. When tradition, culture, and human nature persist in putting someone other than Christ in place of Christ, everyone suffers.

There is considerable consternation and hand-wringing over the identity and work of pastors. "Pastoring is a complicated calling," writes New Testament scholar Scot McKnight, made "endlessly complicated" by "the complexity of the human person."[12] If we were to spend a day with Jesus or Paul, or John or Peter, McKnight insists, we would see firsthand the "unpredictable, wild complication at the heart of the pastoral calling."[13] McKnight believes that the modern era has only made it more complicated because of the myriad of expectations placed on pastors and because of the exposed complexities of the human person.

"Pastoring," McKnight calculates, "is between ten and twelve times more complicated than professoring."[14] It is especially interesting that McKnight believes that "Barth lived in a time when the pastor's calling was far less complicated." In fact, McKnight insists that "the life of the pastor" is four times more complicated today than in Barth's day.[15] This is a surprising observation given that Barth taught theology in Nazi Germany and identified with the Confessing Church until he was forced to return to his native

---

12   McKnight, *Pastor Paul*, 2.
13   McKnight, *Pastor Paul*, 2.
14   McKnight, *Pastor Paul*, 3.
15   McKnight, *Pastor Paul*, 3.

Switzerland. It is hard to imagine that being a pastor in the Chicago suburbs is four times more complicated than opposing Hitler.

McKnight is right in one sense: we live in an age of radical pluralism, characterized by confusion, complexity, disorientation, and decadence. Yet, the world has always been a challenge for the people of God to navigate with the gospel. The absence of the Christendom consensus may actually highlight the meaning of the gospel and Jesus's kingdom ethic more clearly. As the contrast between Christ and the culture becomes starker, the voice of the gospel grows more distinct. Human nature and evil have always been complex, and they have always required a gospel response. But instead of exhausting ourselves on human complexity and the world's confusion, we look to Christ and his Word.

Pastoral ministry does not *react* to the world; it *responds* to the world with the Word of God. Pastors are not called to invent new ways of dealing with people's evolving problems. We are not inno-vators; we are proclaimers. Pastors are called to proclaim the gospel with all the wisdom and energy Christ gives them. The challenge is great, and maybe, at times, overwhelming, but the pastor's job description is not confusing and complex. Our mission is what it has always been: to share the gospel of Jesus Christ. I suspect that if we hung out with Jesus or the apostles, as Scot McKnight suggests, we would discover the clarity and power of the gospel.

McKnight draws out the difference between pastors and pro-fessors. He wonders whether he "could handle the pastor's hand-holding and routine visitations." Since pastors are people-oriented and professors are not, McKnight adds, "Pastors who pastor people have my admiration for their pastoring."[16] To illustrate the "pastoral moment of pastoring real people" McKnight quotes P. D. James's description of pastoral ministry in *Death in Holy Orders*:

[The pastor] had returned from two hours of visiting long-term sick and housebound parishioners. As always

16   McKnight, *Pastor Paul*, 192.

he had tried conscientiously to meet their individual and predictable needs: blind Mrs. Oliver, who liked him to read a passage of scripture and pray with her; old Sam Possinger, who on every visit re-fought the Battle of Al-amein; Mrs. Poley, caged in her Zimmer frame, avid for the latest parish gossip; Carl Lomas, who had never set foot in St. Botolph's but liked discussing theology and the defects of the Church of England.[17]

McKnight portrays quintessential Christendom moments of pas-toring over tea and gingerbread to illustrate the perceived pastoral responsibility to nurture. His impressionistic portrait of the parish priest in a nominally Christian, quaint English village hardly cap-tures the reality of pastoral ministry in our post-Christian, secular age. He calls this "nurturing Christoformity," but it is hard to see how these visits nurture Christlike character, and it is even harder to see "Pastor Paul" fitting this description of pastoral ministry. Paul wrestled with the pastoral expectations and the aggressive moves of the super apostles in Corinth; he debated the metanar-rative of salvation history with the Stoics and Epicureans on Mars hill. These descriptions offer a better picture of pastoral ministry. Any attempt at pastoral theology today that frames the pastor as the congregation's primary hand-holder has missed the mark of a biblical pastoral theology. Relational needs are important and need to be met, but they must be met in a biblical way by the whole household of faith.

The P. D. James description does not fit the apostle Paul's rela-tional pastoral model. I don't picture Paul as excelling in the min-istry of small talk and prepackaged prayers. Paul's daily concern for the churches (2 Cor. 11:28) and his warnings with tears (Acts 20:31) imply an urgency and an intensity that does not fit the polite, patient parish priest. Nor was Paul such a great listener, if we understand

---

17   McKnight, *Pastor Paul*, 192. Quoted from P. D. James, *Death in Holy Orders* (New York: Knopf, 2001), 166.

such a trait to entail hearing each member's concern. Paul wasn't invited to house churches to listen to people's problems but to teach and to preach. I doubt that Paul would have made a particularly good mayoral pastor. From Paul's self-description, I picture him as warm, humble, kind, and approachable, but not overly solicitous of interpersonal niceties. His priority was the gospel of Jesus Christ, and to that end he gave himself without reserve. I picture him fully engaged in dialogue and debate about the truth of the gospel with heartfelt and earnest concern for the listener.

# CHAPTER 9

# ALL WISDOM

*He is the one we proclaim, admonishing and teaching everyone with all wisdom. . . . Let the message of Christ dwell among you richly as you teach and admonish one another with all wisdom through psalms, hymns, and songs from the Spirit, singing to God with gratitude in your hearts.*

—Colossians 1:28; 3:16

A pastoral theology for the household of faith includes the whole counsel of God. This is the truth that is true for everyone everywhere and in every way. To proclaim, admonish, and teach with all wisdom means that the fear of the Lord applies to every aspect of life. This is the wisdom that is necessary for health and wholeness, for personal well-being, and for a flourishing family life. This is the open secret to the integrity and the harmony of the fellowship of believers. This is the wisdom that we take everywhere we go, a wisdom that knows no boundaries and suffers no restrictions. This is the wisdom that applies to the physical side of spirituality and the spiritual side of physicality. John Stott articulates it beautifully: "Our neighbor is neither a bodyless soul that we should love only his soul, nor a soulless body that we should care for its welfare, alone, nor even a body-soul isolated from society. God created man, who is my neighbor, a body-soul-in-community."[1]

Fear-of-the-Lord wisdom is grounded in three interactive elements: the revelation of God, the witness of Christian thought, and the fallen world of human brokenness and suffering.[2] It is obvious that the way the Bible, tradition, and culture interact is complex and ever-changing. The Word of the Lord never changes, it endures forever, but its application is dynamic. It is always directed to a moving target. We need the Holy Spirit, fervent prayer, and the mind of Christ to apply the Word of God well, to truly hear Christ's witness in tradition, and to discern the way of redemption in a fallen world. Each element requires a love that abounds "in knowledge and depth of insight" (Phil. 1:9). There is a right way and a wrong way to believe in the Bible; there is a right way and a wrong way to follow Christian tradition; and there is a right way and a wrong way to interact with culture.

That's what makes living for Christ difficult and complicated and in need of fear-of-the-Lord wisdom. Instead of the Word of God dwelling in us richly it is possible for the Bible to be exploited for our own selfish ends. Sadly, belief that the Bible is inerrant does not prevent it from being used to defend slavery, hypernationalism, xenophobia, exploitation of the poor, and righteousness based upon good works.

The witness of Christian thought is an incalculable blessing. We preach the gospel today with the inspiration and wisdom of early church theologians, the Reformers, and centuries of evangelical thought and witness. Many of the doctrinal issues and heretical threats we face today have been faithfully challenged in earlier eras of church history. We continue to benefit from "such a great cloud of witnesses" (Heb. 12:1). But tradition unchecked

---

1    John Stott, *Christian Mission in the Modern World* (Downers Grove, IL: InterVarsity Press, 1976), 29–30.
2    Graham A. Cole, *Faithful Theology: An Introduction* (Wheaton, IL: Crossway, 2020).

by faithful biblical interpretation leads to distortions and excesses. The Levitical priesthood was never intended to be the prototype of New Testament pastoral ministry, nor was the tabernacle in the wilderness or the temple in Jerusalem meant to model Christian cathedrals. The book of Hebrews calls for a decisive end to religion. Hebrews demonstrates not only the inability of the covenant given at Sinai to atone for sins but the impossibility of any sacerdotal priest, other than Jesus Christ, to atone for sins.[3] The tradition of religions *about* God cannot compare to the tradition of the communion of saints through a personal relationship with the triune God, Father, Son, and Holy Spirit. Jaroslav Pelikan said it well: "Tradition is the living faith of the dead, traditionalism is the dead faith of the living."[4]

We cannot isolate the Bible and Christian tradition from interaction with a fallen and broken world. The New Testament frames the church as salt and light in a decaying and darkening world, as chosen exiles and resident aliens in a world that is not their home, and as the people of God, who are signed, sealed, and delivered. Christians who believe they can wrestle the world into moral conformity with the law of God through political action and legislation fail to comprehend the true power of the gospel to redeem fallen humanity. Christendom in America operates with the misguided notion of American exceptionalism and nationalism. America is not a Christian nation. The fight is not to take back America and make it great again. The fight is to live like Jesus and the early church in a radically pluralistic culture. Cultural Christianity has a way of destroying the Christian witness. Now more than ever we need the household of faith to be outposts of hope in the world for Christ and his kingdom.

---

3    Peter T. O'Brien, *The Letter to the Hebrews*, The Pillar New Testament Commentary (Grand Rapids: Eerdmans, 2010), 482.
4    Jaroslav Pelikan, *The Christian Tradition*, vol. 1 (Chicago: The University of Chicago Press, 1971), 9.

## "ALL"

When we left our church in San Diego to teach in a seminary after fourteen years of pastoral ministry, we received a framed picture of the church with Paul's mission statement from Colossians scripted below in beautiful calligraphy by an artist in our congregation. It was a great gift, designed and made by one of the most thoughtful saints I know. There was only one problem: she forgot the little word "all" in the phrase "with *all* wisdom." At first, the omission bothered me, but now I'm reminded of the need for *all* wisdom every time I look at it.

The implications of this "all-ness" are significant. For the household of faith to embrace the all-encompassing reality of "all wisdom" means thinking Christianly about everything. Harry Blamires, in *The Christian Mind,* laments the church's "abdication of intellectual authority," which led to "the modern Christian's easy descent into mental secularism."[5] Blamires writes, "We have too readily equated getting into the world with getting out of theology. The result has been that we have stopped thinking Christianly." Christianity has been "emasculated of its intellectual relevance," convictions are looked upon as "personal possession," and we have been reduced to encountering one another on the shallow level of gossip and small talk.[6]

Pastors may think Christianly about Sunday's sermon, but when it comes to hiring a worship leader, administrating the building fund, or negotiating salaries they tend to think secularly. Christians have grown so accustomed to secular thinking that they are not even aware that it is secular. Christians who think sexual immorality is a sin but refuse to take a stand publicly because it may offend people are thinking secularly. Blamires offers a further example, noting it is commonplace for believers to "treat worldly possessions as status

---

5     Harry Blamires, *The Christian Mind* (London: SPCK, 1963), 4.
6     Blamires, *The Christian Mind*, 38; see also 13, 16, 40.

symbols rather than as serviceable goods."[7] We don't even bother to think Christianly about war, politics, advertising, sports, business, education, marriage, or divorce.

The apostle Paul framed the issue for the church at Corinth well when he asked, "Where is the wise person? Where is the teacher of the law? Where is the philosopher of this age? Has not God made foolish the wisdom of the world?" (1 Cor. 1:20). Followers of Jesus do not expect the message of the cross to impress the social and cultural elite. Then and now, the intelligentsia reject the metanar-rative of salvation history and the revelational epistemology of the Christian mind.

But the apostle's critique of social status was never an argument against thinking. Christians may not be "wise by human standards," nor influential in the eyes of the world, but the apostle Paul does not use this to disparage the importance of the mind. On the contrary, Paul said, "God chose the foolish things of the world to shame the wise" (1 Cor. 1:27). In Christ, the mind realizes its true significance not as a capacity for self-advancement and self-expression, but as a gift to be developed and disciplined for the sake of the truth. The importance of the mind challenges all believers to rigorous rethinking of their understanding of life and its purpose in accord with the person and work of Christ.

"All wisdom" is the truth that must be embraced by all who de-sire to please God because God's holy claim rests equally on all.[8] This is the all-ness celebrated in Jesus's parable of the hidden treasure: "The kingdom of heaven is like treasure hidden in a field. When a man found it, he hid it again, and then in his joy went and sold all he had and bought that field" (Matt. 13:44). In Christ, this is the *all* that believes that Jesus accomplished *all* on the cross. And this is the *all* that says, "I want to know Christ—yes, to know the power of his resurrection and participation in his sufferings, becoming

---

7    Blamires, *The Christian Mind*, 29.
8    See Douglas D. Webster, *Soundtrack of the Soul: The Beatitudes of Jesus* (To-ronto: Clements, 2009), 90–93.

like him in his death, and so, somehow, to attain to the resurrection from the dead" (Phil. 3:10–11). This is the *all* that inspires believers to rid themselves "of *all* malice and *all* deceit, hypocrisy, envy, and slander of every kind" (1 Peter 2:1, emphasis mine).

This is the *all* of covenant love that is grandly inclusive of *all* we are and will be. This is an *all*-encompassing, timeless commitment. This is the *all* that knows no limits on devotion and righteousness because "against such there is no law" (Gal. 5:23). King David expressed his heartfelt longing when he said, "One thing I ask from the Lord, this only do I seek: that I may dwell in the house of the Lord *all the days of my life*, to gaze on the beauty of the Lord and to seek him in his temple" (Ps. 27:4, emphasis mine). This is the *all* that gives light to our vision of God. Without it we are in darkness, but with it everything is brought into the light.

This is what it means to teach and admonish *with all wisdom*. It is the wisdom of God, not the "wisdom" of the world. It is the wisdom that affirms "not by might nor by power, but by my Spirit" (Zech. 4:6). It is the wisdom that agrees with the psalmist, "Unless the Lord builds the house, the builders labor in vain" (Ps. 127:1).

## CULTURAL TENSIONS AND FULL MATURITY

Applying the whole counsel of God to the wholeness of life requires that our preaching and teaching address the full range of societal issues. Pastoral ministry is more focused on disciple-making in the household of faith than it is in Christendom. Christ's followers must address the issues: from wealth and poverty, race and class, science and faith, sexuality and marriage, creation care and the environment, social justice and politics, gun control and immigration, nationalism and globalization, food security and diet, to health care and education. We need to proclaim the gospel, preach the prophets, pray the Psalms, apply the Sermon on the Mount, and practice New Testament spiritual direction.

Cultural Christianity, characterized by Kierkegaard as Christianity without Christ, reduces spirituality to the existential self.

Christendom, either of the liberal left or the conservative right, reinforces individualism and understands religion as a private affair. If our Christianity is to be with Christ, we must ask ourselves what it means to plant the cross of Jesus Christ in the middle of a pandemic or in the midst of racial tension. The church cannot remain silent when people suffer injustice, when they are denied human rights, and when authoritarian governments usurp the authority of Christ.

The apostle Paul raised the bar for the household of faith in a way we can hardly imagine today. His stated goal was to teach *everyone* with all wisdom so that *we* may present *everyone fully* mature in Christ. Churches set goals all the time, but not this one: to present "everyone fully mature in Christ." We hear just the opposite. Believers say in all sincerity, "I just want a simple faith. Just give me Jesus." What they really mean is, "I don't want the responsibility of growing in the grace and knowledge of the Lord Jesus Christ." They have no intention of becoming like Jesus. They don't want to be bothered by the complexity of evil. They are not impressed by the emotional range of the Psalms with its high praise and moral pain. They're not interested in Jesus's kingdom ethic or in vocational holiness or in God's mission for the global church.

Professing Christians who have attended church for decades and listened to countless sermons are unable to articulate their faith in Christ. Psalm 23 is their favorite psalm, and they have John 3:16 memorized and they think and act like their "secular" neighbor. They have been told over and over to believe in Jesus and they do, but their reasons for faith date back to their youth, with little sign of maturation. They suffer from a case of *PSA—perpetual spiritual adolescence*.

## ENVY AND EQUALITY

Splitting the restaurant check fifty-fifty doesn't seem fair when your friend orders a thirty-dollar steak and you order an eight-dollar salad. Treating everyone the same can be an excuse for avoiding the challenging work of assessing need and recognizing worth. In order to be fair, we treat our three children differently: their individual needs and circumstances require distinct kinds of support. Instead of a leveling response designed to preserve a semblance of fairness, we endeavor to show *equal concern for each of them* by responding to them differently. This requires wisdom and discernment beyond a simple understanding of equity. It would be easier, but not as wise, to treat our children the same.

"Equal concern for each other" (1 Cor. 12:25) in the household of faith does not mean all should be treated the same. Everyone ought to be loved to the same extent, but served in specific ways according to their needs. Differences in maturity, commitment, Spirit gifts, and responsibility demand that the leadership engage in prayerful discernment (Phil. 1:9–11) to strive for the greatest benefit to the ministry and mission of the body of Christ.

The gifts of the Spirit in the life of the church resist the leveling impulse of our democratic individualism. Instead of treating everyone the same, the church recognizes the particular value and unique responsibilities of each individual believer. Everyone is gifted in the Spirit, and the diversity of gifts means the body of Christ "is not made up of one part but of many" (1 Cor. 12:14).

Spiritual leaders (not limited to pastors) need to discriminate in deploying persons in ministry. Leaders should not be *biased*, basing decisions on external factors, such as gender, race, age, appearance, or ambition. Missionaries, pastors, teachers, elders, deacons, and caregivers are not chosen because they represent a constituency in the church or because they aspire for a role to play in the church, but because they are called and gifted by the Lord to fulfill God's mission. Christians are all equally part of the body of Christ, but not all Christians serve the body of Christ in the same way.

An equal-opportunity democracy is a welcome alternative to the social stratification of first-century Roman culture. However, the leveling effect of modern individualism does not invoke the same relational dynamic as the body of Christ's unity in diversity. The early church created a whole new way of living in community that overcame racial, economic, and gender divisions (Gal. 3:28). This was James's concern when he wrote, categorically, "My brothers and sisters, believers in our glorious Lord Jesus Christ must not show favoritism" (James 2:1). James condemned favoring the wealthy over the poor. He favored believers with a working faith and a tamed tongue—who submitted to the wisdom of God.

The apostles taught that life together was rooted in Christ, and everyone was "baptized by one Spirit so as to form one body— whether Jews or Gentiles, slave or free—and we were all given the one Spirit to drink" (1 Cor. 12:13). The apostle Paul qualifies this "oneness" in a distinctive way when he adds, "Even so the body is not made up of one part but of many" (1 Cor. 12:14). And each part of the body was meant to play a significant role in the body. Paul addressed the problem of envy with his famous dialogue between talking body parts.

> Now if the foot should say, "Because I am not a hand, I do not belong to the body," it would not for that reason stop being part of the body.... If the whole body were an eye, where would the sense of hearing be? If the whole body were an ear, where would the sense of smell be? But in fact, God has placed the parts of the body, every one of them, just as he wanted them to be. If they were all one part, where would the body be? As it is, there are many parts, but one body. (1 Cor. 12:15, 17–20)

Unity and diversity within the body of Christ calls for equal concern for each other as well as prayerful discernment. Each of us has different responsibilities in the household of faith.

Of all team sports, soccer may illustrate Paul's emphasis best. There are eleven distinct positions, and each player is expected to play their position. When the team is playing in sync offensively and defensively, it is impressive to see the variety of skills and the beauty of collaboration. Goalkeepers and wingbacks rarely score goals, but they are vital to a winning strategy. The forwards or strikers tend to score the most goals because they are fed the ball by the team.

Paul illustrates envy's thoughtless ways when he says, "The eye cannot say to the hand, 'I don't need you!' And the head cannot say to the feet, 'I don't need you!' On the contrary, those parts of the body that seem to be weaker are indispensable, and the parts that we think are less honorable we treat with special honor" (1 Cor. 12:21–23). We are not all the same, but we should show "equal concern for each other" (12:25). We each have a responsibility within Christ's body and a role to play in God's mission, but it is not the same responsibility for everyone.

## ENVY'S ENERGY

One of the earliest observers of American culture was the French diplomat and philosopher Alexis de Tocqueville. He came to America in the 1830s to better understand the "equality of condition among the people."[9] He commended American culture in many ways, but he noted our propensity to minimize the importance of the mind and gravitate to the lowest common denominator. He claimed that the energy behind this dumbing down and leveling of culture was envy.

De Tocqueville attributed this phenomenon to the general populace's low level of intelligence. He wrote, "It is impossible, after the most strenuous exertions, to raise the intelligence of the people above a certain level. Whatever may be the facilities of acquiring information, whatever may be the profusion of easy methods and cheap science, the human mind can never be instructed and developed without devoting considerable time to these objects."[10] Cultivating intelligence and maturity is challenging enough in a culture of sound-bite tweets, short attention spans, and text messaging, but de Tocqueville described issues that predate our modern ones. Class divisions between the educated and uneducated, between professionals and laborers, he argued, inhibited a commitment to the

---

9  Alexis de Tocqueville, *Democracy in America*, vol. 1 (New York: Vintage, 1945), 3.

10  De Tocqueville, *Democracy in America*, 1:207.

universal education necessary for developing the human capacity for discernment. Americans, he argued, were too easily fooled and beguiled by ideas and politicians because they lacked the critical thinking skills that general education imparts. The energy necessary to become well-informed was replaced by envy.

It is fair to say that de Tocqueville's cultural analysis applies to the evangelical church. Our leveling impulse is evident when preaching serves the lowest common denominator and when our primary goal is to avoid hurting feelings. J. I. Packer summed up North American Protestantism as "man-centered, manipulative, success-oriented, self-indulgent and sentimental. . . . [It is] 3,000 miles wide and half an inch deep."[11] Ironically, preachers blame the shallowness of their sermons on their congregations, and congregations blame their lack of spiritual growth on the predictable, repetitive sermons their pastors deliver. Christians who have pursued highly sophisticated careers in science and industry typically know little more about Jesus's ethic than they did during their high-school years. If we pursued Jesus with the same zeal and devotion we give to fashion, homes, careers, finances, studies, sports, and cars, we might be more mature.

Paul expected all believers to share his clearheaded passion for Christ: "I consider everything a loss compared to the surpassing worth of knowing Christ Jesus my Lord, for whose sake I have lost all things" (Phil. 3:8). If we followed the apostle Paul in this way, we would employ the wide breadth of talent within the body of Christ to plumb in order to share the deep truths of the gospel. The felt need to package the gospel to reach the lowest common denominator is related to the fear of invoking envy by recognizing gifted believers.

De Tocqueville claimed *envy* was the energy of mediocrity. Envy suppresses the quest for intellectual maturity. Envy insists on equal recognition. Among Christians envy mitigates against taking the faith seriously and growing in the grace and knowledge of our Lord Jesus Christ (2 Peter 3:18). In not-so-subtle ways we want "a simple

---

11   Packer, *A Quest for Godliness*, 22.

faith" free from the complexity of thinking Christianly about a full range of issues and responsibilities. We favor treating everyone the same because we do not want to apply ourselves to a love that abounds "more and more in knowledge and depth of insight" (Phil. 1:9). We don't want to feel insecure or inferior around our fellow Christians, but neither do we want to apply ourselves to the diligent work required to grow into maturity. We are more inclined to dumb down the gospel to our comfort level then to accept the impact of the gospel in every area of life and in the full range of ministries.

De Tocqueville claimed that the American experiment in democracy promoted "the feeling of envy in the human heart."[12] Americans, he believed, were offered the advantages of equality and advancement, especially economic advancement, but they were perpetually disappointed. They underestimated the effort and the frustrations involved in achieving social and economic advancement. De Tocqueville's description of American socioeconomic envy holds true for spiritual envy as well. We have every resource available to grow in Christ and serve Christ's body, but the spiritual discipline and drive is not there to acquire "full maturity."

De Tocqueville drew this conclusion about Americans in general: "Whatever transcends their own limitations appears to be an obstacle to their desires, and *there is no superiority, however legitimate it may be, which is not irksome in their sight*."[13] Christians are content to listen to a few celebrity pastors and read a few popular Christian books before concluding that they know enough. They are easily satisfied and convinced that everyone is entitled to their opinion and that no one's view is more important than anyone else's. It seems many Christians don't know how to react to a fellow believer whose "love abounds more and more in knowledge and depth of insight" without feeling intimidated.

American individualism tends to suppress gifted believers and insist that everyone remain at the same level of biblical insight and

---

12  Tocqueville, *Democracy in America*, 1:208.
13  Tocqueville, *Democracy in America*, 1:208 (emphasis mine).

wisdom. Mature Christians tend to be irksome in our sight, especially if they do not hold a leadership office. We are uncomfortable
looking up to mature, older, *ordinary* believers and learning from
them. The cultural commitment to equality and individualism has
resulted in flattening spiritual growth, leveling Christian maturity,
and suppressing gifted service.

Young seminarians confront this reality at the outset of their
ministry. Three to four years of intensive biblical and theological
education does not count for much in the church. In fact, the atti-
tude of some in the church is that they need to teach new ministers
a thing or two about working in the "real world." Ironically, we don't
presume to know the law better than a trained lawyer nor pretend to
know medicine more than a practicing physician, but four years of
studying the Bible, church history and doctrine, Hebrew and Greek,
alongside preaching, pastoral theology, and counseling, often means
little to believers who are suspicious of the mind and sensitive to
feeling inferior. Some believers see theological education as a liability
that fuels pride and destroys a simple faith.

Imagine someone breaking into the wine cellar of a five-star hotel
and in the name of equality removing all the labels from the wine
bottles, making it impossible for anyone to tell the difference between
an expensive vintage wine from a trusted winery and an inexpensive
ordinary wine of unknown origins. I might like the simplified wine
list—let me choose between red and white—but those who know
their wines would be dismayed, even outraged. But when it comes
to the church and ministry, we do much the same thing. We find it
awkward to distinguish between immaturity and maturity, between
foolishness and wisdom. It is easier to lump everyone together in the
name of equality. It takes some knowledge to match the right wine with
certain foods, and it takes some maturity to match the right person
with the gifts and abilities needed for ministry.

Jesus gave only one method of numerical and spiritual church
growth: making disciples. He commissioned the church to "go and
make disciples of all nations . . . [and teach] them to obey everything I have commanded you" (Matt. 28:19–20). The great texts of

Christian responsibility, including the Sermon on the Mount, the Upper Room Discourse, and the Pauline epistles—are all given by the Holy Spirit to equip the people of God "so that the body of Christ may be built up until we all reach unity and in the faith in the knowledge of the Son of God and become mature, attaining to the whole measure of the fullness of Christ" (Eph. 4:12–13). Making disciples involves a deepening desire to grow in the grace and knowledge of Christ. Discernment is required to discriminate and deploy gifted believers in the humbling and exhausting work of making disciples. While we are committed to showing equal concern for one another, we must be able to discern gifts in order to entrust persons with the responsibilities of ministry wisely. In Christ, we seek to curb envy's power to suppress the Spirit's gifts and invoke feelings of inferiority.

In the 1990s, pollster and church growth guru George Barna argued that there are two distinct yet complementary church growth strategies, one for numerical growth and one for spiritual growth. "The tactics required to develop strong spiritual character," Barna reasoned, "are very different from the tactics required to generate numerical growth. Failure to pursue and achieve balance between these competing but complementary interests leads to an unhealthy church."[14] Barna insisted that since we live in a highly competitive, materialistic, secular marketplace that vies for our attention, we need to find ways to appeal to the consumer. He wrote, "My contention, based on careful study of data and the activities of American churches, is that the major problem plaguing the Church is its failure to embrace a marketing orientation in what has become a market-driven environment."[15]

Two decades later Barna predicted "an unprecedented re-engineering of America's faith" due to widespread disillusionment with vision-casting megachurches. A new generation of believers, Barna

---

14  George Barna, *User Friendly Churches* (Ventura, CA: Regal, 1991), 23.
15  George Barna, *Marketing the Church: What They Never Taught You about Church Growth* (Colorado Springs: NavPress, 1988), 23.

observed, "refuse to follow people in ministry leadership positions who cast a personal vision rather than God's, who seek popularity rather than the proclamation of truth in their public statements, or who are more concerned about their own legacy than that of Jesus Christ."[16] Nonetheless, besides failing to acknowledge his complicity in the market-driven church, Barna continues to reject the disciple-making strategy of the early church.

Instead, he calls for new models of "spiritual intimacy" to maximize the individual freedom of believers. He encourages Christians to choose "from a proliferation of options, weaving together a set of favored alternatives into a unique tapestry that constitutes the personal 'church' of the individual."[17] Individual believers ought to embrace the freedom and excitement of doing what they want to do. They decide for themselves what advances the faith for themselves and what meets their personal needs. If playing golf on Sunday lowers their stress and helps them reflect more thoughtfully on the Bible, then skipping corporate worship makes sense. Barna's reasoning is simple enough: *Who needs the hassles of the local church, anyway? The autonomous individual self can be a denomination of one. You can be your own local church.*

It is safe to say that we have focused too much on the individual at the expense of the household of faith. Although the New Testament is mainly addressed to the community of disciples, we have focused our preaching on the individual. We have confused a personal faith with Western individualism. We have catered to the individual consumer and the private religious self. Christians who say they're on fire for Jesus, but don't have a clue as to what Jesus taught in the Sermon on the Mount, are like the seeds thrown on rocky ground (Matt. 13:5). The gospel is meant to impact everything about us, including our social, political, economic, and relational lives.

---

16   George Barna, *Revolution: Finding Vibrant Faith beyond the Walls of the Sanctuary* (Carol Stream, IL: Tyndale, 2006), 14.
17   Barna, *Revolution*, 66.

## BEYOND A SIMPLE FAITH

It is easy to grow naive and complacent behind the walls of our ignorance. We have mastered the art of self-censorship on a host of social and political issues. We have narrowed the gospel down to a private religious experience. And then we wonder why the church is no different from the world. The priestly ministry of the body of Christ moves us into the world on a mission. We are in the world, but not of the world. Each and every believer is called to a holy vocation and together we are called to be a faithful presence in the world. We are ambassadors for Christ, called, not to conform to the world, but to "be transformed by the renewing of [our] mind[s]," so that we will be able "to test and approve what God's will is—his good, pleasing and perfect will" (Rom. 12:2).

To be in the world but not of the world is not easily done. We may take pride in our conservative theology and our staunch moral stand but be downright worldly in our neglect of the poor and in our ambition for wealth. Our doctrinal stance may be conservative, but our devotion to sports and material success may be idolatrous. We may attend Sunday worship services regularly, but do we spend the rest of the week living for ourselves? Do we wrap the cross in the American flag in the name of patriotism? Do we put on a show of traditional piety during Christmas while falling before the idol of materialism?

In *Living in Tension,* I write that the best way to describe a comprehensive and integrative approach to culture is to use the little, flexible, preposition "for." Christ *for* culture includes what Christ opposes in our culture for the sake of redemption and reconciliation. Christ *for* culture underscores the love and compassion that Christ and his followers demonstrate on behalf of culture. If Christ is *for* culture, who can be against it? The ultimate victory of the risen Lord Jesus Christ is assured, having conquered sin and death and overcome the devil and his forces. No one has the power to impact culture positively and transform its members but Christ alone. Christ is *for* culture, as Creator, Savior, reigning Lord, and coming King.

Christians who take the Bible seriously and believe in the Lordship of Jesus Christ embrace the Bible as their countercultural guide. The prophets and the apostles become their faithful and effective witnesses to gospel living. They no longer equate Christianity with civil religion and American exceptionalism. For them the kingdom of God has little to do with the American dream. Biblical Christians are for the unborn, the refugee, the poor, and the sinner. We are for racial justice and social righteousness. We proclaim an inclusive gospel with an exclusive truth claim. Jesus Christ is the way, the truth, and the life. We seek to evangelize the lost. We believe in heaven and hell. We believe in gender differentiation rooted in God's biological law. We are committed to sexual purity and marital fidelity between a man and a woman. We are pro-life, pro-marriage, and pro-immigrant, but not in a way that imposes our will on the culture. Humanity, male and female, is made in God's image (Gen. 1:27). In concert with the Bible's understanding of human persons, we believe that one's manhood or womanhood constitutes a holistic biological and spiritual dimension bestowed by God at conception (Gen. 1:27; Jer. 1:5). The Bible considers sex to be biologically established. Personal identity is a divine gift. It summons us to its gendered expression in light of its biological reality. While the body matters to our personal identity, the most important thing that can be said about our personal identity is that we are made in God's image and redeemed by Christ alone.

We work for the common good and charitable civility, but we cannot legislate the moral order of the church in a pluralistic state. We may suffer society's persecution, but we cannot make society into our image. The New Testament epistle of 1 Peter is a straightforward guide for today's Christian living in a culture that is in many ways antithetical to the gospel. We are "resident aliens" and "chosen exiles" living for Christ in our home culture. For the Christian, life is lived "back to the future": we are ready to make a costly commitment, following the example of Christians in the early church. We are for the world the way Christ was for the world. We need pastoral leaders who will help us disentangle true biblical convictions from the strategies and behaviors of the world.

Distinguished Cambridge historian Sir Herbert Butterfield's 1949 publication of *Christianity and History* envisioned the future of Christianity in the light of its past:

> After a period of fifteen hundred years or so we can just about begin to say that at last no one is now a Christian because of government compulsion, or because it is the way to procure favor at court, or because it is necessary to qualify for public office, or because he would lose customers if he did not go to church, or even because habit and intellectual indolence keep the mind in the appointed groove. . . . We are back for the first time in something like the earliest centuries of Christianity, and those early centuries afford some relevant clues to the kind of attitude to adopt.[18]

For those who think the future of Christianity is bleak, it is encouraging to compare Herbert Butterfield's assessment of Christianity's future with the Letter to Diognetus, a second-century description of Christian life:

> Christians are distinguished from other people neither by country, nor language, nor the customs which they observe. . . . They dwell in their own countries, but simply as sojourners. As citizens they share in all things with others, and yet endure all things as if foreigners. Every foreign land is to them as their native country, and every land of their birth as a land of strangers. They marry, as do all; they beget children; but they do not destroy their offspring. They have a common table, but not a common bed. They are in the flesh, but they do not live after the flesh. They pass their days on earth, but they are citizens of heaven. They obey the prescribed laws,

---

18   Herbert Butterfield, *Christianity and History* (New York: Scribner, 1950), 135.

and at the same time surpass the laws by their lives. They love all people and are persecuted by all. They are unknown and condemned. . . . They are poor, yet make many rich. . . . They are dishonored, and yet in their very dishonor are glorified. They are evil spoken of, and yet are justified; they are reviled and bless; they are insulted, and repay the insult with honor; they do good, yet are punished as evil doers.[19]

## THE JUDGMENT OF GOD

A friend who is an architect in Hong Kong shared with me a conversation that he had with an investment banker from Taiwan who worked in New York City. The banker volunteered that the profits made in investment banking through collateralized debt obligations and credit default swaps were obscene and unconscionable. Sensing that he was open, my friend challenged him: "Are those who engineered these profits guilty of sin? Are Christian bankers not only culpable but guilty of an idolatrous relationship with the financial system?" The Christian banker maintained that the system was "neutral" and that its globalization had led to explosive prosperity around the world. Then, my friend went deeper and asked what will Jesus say when Christian bankers and brokers stand before him in the judgment?

I am convicted by my friend's question, because I confess Christ's judgment does not have the impact on my thinking and actions nearly as much as it should. To be honest, I tend to view the final judgment as nothing to worry about because Christ has saved me from my sins. The book of Revelation describes "a great white throne" at the end of history (Rev. 20:11). Yet the apostle Paul painted a sobering picture when he described a believer's life's

---

19  Quoted in R. E. O. White, *Christian Ethics* (Philadelphia: John Knox, 1981), 20.

work destroyed in the judgment. In Paul's analogy, the believer used inferior building materials, though he built on the foundation of Jesus Christ.

My wife and I regularly walk through an adjacent neighborhood where the houses were built with defective drywall. The walls of these homes contain extraneous metals and minerals, such as sulfur, strontium, and iron, and in our warm, humid climate the drywall emits sulfur gasses. We have seen beautiful homes that needed to be gutted, stripped down to the studs, and rebuilt from the inside out because they were built with contaminated sheetrock. Likewise, many churches look good on the outside, but inside they contain worldly perceptions and ideologies that overtime destroy the impact of the Word of God and the witness of the church.

Paul warned, "the builder will suffer loss but yet will be saved—even though only as one escaping through the flames" (1 Cor. 3:15). This graphic picture of a believer's life work going up in smoke as he runs for his life is in tension with Paul's positive picture of competing in the race to receive a crown that will last forever: "I don't know about you," Paul urges, "but I'm running hard for the finish line. I'm giving it everything I've got. No lazy living for me! I'm staying alert and in top condition. I'm not going to get caught napping, telling everyone else all about it and then missing out myself" (1 Cor. 9:26–27 MSG).

Competing for the victory crown, which is described as the crown of life, signifying victory over death (James 1:12; Rev. 2:10); or the crown of righteousness, signifying victory over sin (2 Tim. 4:8); or the crown of glory, signifying victory over all that is passing away (1 Peter 5:4) has nothing to do with works righteousness or self-righteousness, but everything to do with "fixing our eyes on Jesus, the pioneer and perfecter of faith. For the joy set before him he endured the cross, scorning its shame, and sat down at the right hand of the throne of God" (Heb. 12:2). This is the crown worth investing in. You can bank on it.

Christian martyr Dietrich Bonhoeffer highlighted this difference when he compared the costly grace of Jesus Christ with the cheap grace of religious conformity and nominal Christianity. To tell believers week after week that "there is now no condemnation for those who are in Christ Jesus" (Rom. 8:1), without explaining and expounding on what it means to be in Christ Jesus, may have the unintended effect of condoning and enabling believers who are far more conformed to this world than transformed by Christ.

The sober side of hope finds far more expression in the New Testament than we often admit. Saving faith cannot be separated from a serving faith. Jesus said, "For the Son of Man is going to come in his Father's glory with his angels, and then he will reward each person according to what they have done" (Matt. 16:27; see also Rom. 2:6). True faith is always a working faith. "So, we make it our goal to please him," declared the apostle Paul, "whether we are at home in the body or away from it. For we must all appear before the judgment seat of Christ, so that each of us may receive what is due us for the things done while in the body, whether good or bad" (2 Cor. 5:9–10).

## THE *ECCLESIA* ECOSYSTEM

The process of creating a household of faith *in the Spirit* with our pastoral fathers and mothers needs an "organic, hands-on, and communal approach to knowing."[20] Theological and relational depth are not entrepreneurial products engineered by following the latest formulas and recipes for success. Spiritual depth results from the slow work of life-on-life, loving discipleship. Growing the household of faith involves life-changing devotion to Christ, manifest in a commitment to "the apostles' teaching and to fellowship, to the breaking of bread and to prayer" (Acts 2:42). The Spirit leads us to the rich soil of salvation history and church history, creating an ecosystem that sustains the fellowship of Jesus. The rhythms of grace in worship and in ordinary life are cultivated, young people are nurtured in the fear and admonition of the Lord, critical thinking

---

20  Fujimura, *Art and Truth*, 37.

skills are sharpened, holy vocations are celebrated, and the mission of God is embraced.

This kind of ecosystem does not necessitate a small church. The early church exploded in size at Pentecost; nonetheless, the church maintained its commitment to the four key fundamentals expressed in Acts 2:42: proclamation of the whole counsel of God, genuine fellowship and friendship in Christ, holy communion with the triune God, and heartfelt, prayerful discernment. This ecosystem is not maintained by church size, whether small or big, but by devotion to the apostles' teaching and to a body of believers, believers who behave as Christ's disciples. They practice living the resurrection.

Every cell in the body needs a fresh supply of oxidized blood and every member of the body of Christ needs to be a part of the Holy Spirit's circulation system. It is important that churches start right and stay right so that their ecclesial DNA reflects the essential elements of the New Testament church. We can't afford to buy into a secular crowd-pleasing marketing strategy. Neither can we cling to our religious traditions to preserve our cherished culture. We operate with a biblical set of principles designed to grow the church spiritually and numerically. The Bible remains the touchstone for everything we do.

Churches that stay within their financial means underscore their dependence on the Lord. Neither money nor the spirit of the times are meant to drive the energy of the church. Numbers become a liability when a church longs for a charismatic power figure and pastoral ego to run the place. When the household of faith is minimized and institutional power and preservation are maximized, cultural religion replaces true faith with comfortable complacency. Meaningful fellowship and sacrificial faithfulness are lost in a religious culture of conformity and passivity. Whatever size the household of faith, the church thrives when the gospel of grace is embraced, the whole counsel of God is taught, and Christ's kingdom is sought. The beauty of the *ecclesia* ecosystem is manifest in the proclamation and practice of God's Word.

# CHAPTER 10

# TO THIS END

*To this end I strenuously contend with all the energy Christ so powerfully works in me.*

—Colossians 1:29

*What in the ministry is satisfaction? Do the prophets and apostles, not to speak of Jesus Christ, give us the impression of being people who have succeeded, who could at the end look back upon a blessed and satisfying life? Strange that we do so much better than they? What can it mean? It means above all that we should feel a fundamental alarm.*

—Karl Barth[1]

U nlearning the Christendom model of pastoral ministry and embracing the early church's New Testament model of pastoral ministry involves a significant transvaluation of priorities and concerns. The apostle Paul's sharp break from religious self-confidence to Christian confidence helps to illustrate the transformation of the church from a Christendom model

---

1    Karl Barth, *The Word of God and The Word of Man*, trans. by Douglas Horton (Cleveland, OH: Pilgrim, 1928), 125.

to the model of the household of faith. Paul's understanding of religious power, privilege, and purpose changed radically when he met the risen Lord Jesus. Before Christ, Paul's world revolved around institutional self-preservation, group or tribal identity, personal ambition, professional credentials, passionate zeal, and religious pride. After his Damascus road experience, he evaluated all of his prior religious gains and priorities as a total loss for the sake of Christ (Phil. 3:4–11). His passion shifted from religion to knowing Christ and the power of his resurrection and the fellowship of his suffering.

There will always be the need to unlearn the processes that rob pastoral ministry and the fellowship of Jesus of the abundant life rooted in the gospel (John 10:10). The temptation to fixate on budgets, buildings, and credentials, as we strive to please passive recipients of spiritual services will remain. It will always be easier to be driven by consumer demand and the insatiable therapeutic needs of the admirers of Jesus who have no intention of taking up their cross and following Jesus. It will always be easier to put charismatic personalities in positions of power to preserve the church.

Embracing pastoral ministry in the household of faith places us on a steep learning curve. The apostle Paul stated the end, or goal, of this learning curve succinctly, to proclaim Christ and make disciples. As such, we, like Paul, are committed to a life of obedience. The fruit-bearing life of the church cannot be preserved through institutional safeguards, organizational efficiencies, worldly leadership, and pastoral authority. The health and holiness of the body of Christ require the integration of all the bodily systems for the purpose of proclaiming Christ and making disciples. This requires the fullness of the Holy Spirit, the proclamation of the whole counsel of God, the active participation of the priesthood of all believers, our mutual submission in Christ, humble authority from pastoral leadership, a plurality of mature spiritual leaders, and Christ-centered worship.

"Today we emphasize the New Birth," writes Peter Gillquist. "The ancients emphasized being faithful to the end. We moderns talk of wholeness and purposeful living; they spoke of the glories of the eternal kingdom. . . . The emphasis in our attention has shifted from the completing of the Christian life to the beginning of it."[2] The apostle Paul was committed, as we should be, to the whole spectrum of gospel ministry from proclaiming Christ to presenting everyone fully mature in Christ. The household of faith is faithful to both evangelism and edification in order "to equip his people for works of service, so that the body of Christ may be built up until we all reach unity in the faith and knowledge of the Son of God and become mature, attaining to the whole measure of the fullness of Christ" (Eph. 4:12–13).

## RESPONSIBILITY AND ACCOUNTABILITY

The apostle's mission statement emphasizes two important truths: there is a plurality of responsibility and a singularity of accountability. He writes, "*we* proclaim . . . so that *we* may present everyone fully mature in Christ" (Col. 1:28, emphasis mine). While acknowledging he works alongside others in proclaiming the gospel, Paul nonetheless takes personal responsibility for his own calling: "To this end *I* strenuously contend with all the energy Christ so powerfully works in *me*" (Col. 1:29, emphasis mine). In Paul's mind there is balance and synergy between plurality and singularity. We were meant to work together. We cannot do it alone, and our partnership in the gospel was from the beginning until now (Phil. 1:5). There never was a time when we did this on our own, without the fellowship of believers, without mutual submission, without shared responsibility, without every-member ministry. A congregation of persons undergoing discipleship and making disciples are responsible for shaping pastoral identity and not the other way around. This plurality of responsibility runs against the deeply ingrained American habit of individualism. Our culture celebrates personal recognition, individual competition, and singular leadership. We

---

2     Peter Gillquist, "A Marathon We Are Meant to Win," *Christianity Today,* October 23, 1981, 22.

are wired *culturally* to coalesce around a charismatic, larger-than-life personality. But the Bible teaches us to live together in mutual submission to Christ. The New Testament celebrates the fellowship of believers as "a chosen people, a royal priesthood, a holy nation, God's special possession" (1 Peter 2:9).

Where does that leave the individual? Paul uses himself as an example. He is accountable for himself, just as each and every believer is accountable for themselves. He cannot make the commitment for us, but we can learn from him and benefit from his example. His testimony is clear, "To this end *I* strenuously contend . . .". It is not his job to browbeat believers into a greater commitment. He doesn't guilt them into submission. But he does expect that the joy and privilege of his commitment to Christ and the gospel will have an impact on others. He hopes that they will identity with him so that they can say with him, "I became a servant of this gospel by the gift of God's grace given me through the working of his power" (Eph. 3:7); or, "I am what I am" only by God's grace, "and his grace to me was not without effect" (1 Cor. 15:10); or, "I strenuously contend with all the energy Christ so powerful works in me" (Col. 1:29).

Responsibility is shared; accountability is real. By God's grace the church doesn't take advantage of the individual, nor does the individual take advantage of the church. The synergy between the plurality of responsibility and the singularity of accountability works to the mutual benefit of the body of Christ. Instead of Christendom, in which the pastor ministers to passive recipients of spiritual services, it is a household of faith in which a plurality of spiritual leaders and a pastoral team endeavor to build up one another in Christ. This person-to-person, in-community model is one where responsibilities are shared, which, in turn, inspires personal accountability.

## A SHARED WORK ETHIC

Like Paul, pastors lead the household of faith by their positive example of hard work and costly commitment, but this commitment is not in lieu of a true partnership in the gospel within the church. Sometimes congregations hide behind a double standard in order to justify inadequate compensation for their pastors. They reason that since pastors are more committed than laypeople, they can afford to pay them less. The double standard also justifies complacency and passivity. This kind of reasoning meets its challenge in the New Testament's unequivocal emphasis on a shared workload.

In some Christian circles "striving" is a bad word because it is alleged that our *effort* mitigates against God's grace. The apostles disagree: they refused to confuse the work of righteousness with a righteousness based upon works. They accepted the challenge of the Sermon on the Mount. Jesus's disciple-making instruction was not given to the church to prove its impossibility, as if to say, "You can't do what is taught here, only Christ can do it." By God's grace, disciples are empowered to love instead of hate, to practice purity instead of lust, fidelity instead of infidelity, honesty instead of dishonesty, reconciliation instead of retaliation, and prayer instead of revenge. Jesus did not teach the Sermon on the Mount to prove how inadequate we are to save ourselves; he taught the Sermon on the Mount to prove the difference salvation makes in our daily lives because of Christ.

Luther was right: "Our striving would be losing, if the right Man were not on our side," but the right man *is* on our side, and we are inspired and empowered by Christ to live the gospel life. When Paul writes, "For to me, to live is Christ and to die is gain," or "I press on toward the goal to win the prize for which God has called me heavenward in Christ Jesus" (Phil. 1:21; 3:14), he has every expectation that fellow believers will echo this passion for Christ. When he writes, "Continue to work out your salvation with fear and trembling, for it is God who works in you to will and to act in order to fulfill his good purpose," Paul is right there alongside the body of Christ working out his own salvation (Phil. 2:12–13). "We labor and strive," Paul insisted, "because we have put our hope in the living God, who is the Savior of all people" (1 Tim. 4:10).

When the apostles urged believers to "make every effort to add to your faith goodness; and to goodness, knowledge; and to knowledge, self-control; and to self-control, perseverance; and to perseverance, godliness; and to godliness, mutual affection; and to mutual affection, love," they were describing the profile of a priest in the priesthood of all believers. Every believer, pastor included, is urged to "make every effort to confirm [one's] calling and election" (2 Peter 1:5–7, 10).

## STRATEGIES OF RENEWAL

Paul's purpose could not be clearer: he proclaims Christ and further disciples those who accept this proclamation in order that he may "present everyone fully mature in Christ" (Col. 1:28). And what was true for Paul should be true for us. To that end Paul "strenuously" contended with "all the energy Christ so powerfully worked" in him (Col. 1:29). The Message translation reads, "That's what I'm working so hard at day after day, year after year, doing my best with the energy God so generously gives me" (Col. 1:29 MSG). This demanding work is not to be confused with the busy pastor who spends his or her days hassled and hurried, running from one appointment to another and from one committee to another. The daily routine of pastors reflects their passions and priorities. If the passion and priority is to run the church, it won't be long before the pastor is run-down. If it is all about serving the church in the Jesus way, hopefully, it won't be long before people begin to change their expectations. But, pastors and laypeople alike are addicted to the workaholic pastor. The omnicompetent pastor in a Christendom church may be successful in organizing and administering complex systems. He may be good at raising money, hiring and managing staff, vision-casting for the future, and performing well on Sunday. But these leadership competencies are not what the apostle had in mind when he described himself as working hard, day after day, year after year. Paul envisioned leadership in the tradition of Jesus, work that required Christ's energy to carry out. The Christendom legacy must be unlearned, and the Jesus way must be learned.

Rhythms of grace inspire disciplined devotion and prayer, reading and studying, physical exercise and good eating habits, along with rest and relaxation. Time is set aside for counseling and relating, worship planning and sermon preparation, along with attending to the needs of others. These daily rhythms are a form of spiritual discipline that help sustain pastoral ministry. And these daily, sustainable patterns lead to decades of meaningful pastoral leadership. It is important for the pastoral team and for spiritual leaders in the church to set an example for the household of faith in how they organize their ordinary, daily routine and use it for the glory of God. By way of contrast, living the daily grind robs Christians of ordinary joy and sets them up for disappointment.

Psychoanalyst Herbert Freudenberger defines a burnout as "someone in a state of fatigue or frustration brought about by devotion to a cause, way of life, or relationship that failed to produce the expected reward."[3] Exhausted pastors, weary with stale patterns of church routine, are ready to chuck it all and head in the opposite direction. Nothing on their calendar interests them. Even positive validation from members no longer means much. They are tired of hearing the sound of their own voice. And they don't have a clue as to how to reboot and start fresh.

I remember the Easter that I hit the wall. I was pastoring a small urban church in Toronto and teaching theology. We had three children under five and it seemed like I was working twenty-four seven. That Easter morning, I stood before the congregation sleep deprived and exhausted. I gave the traditional call to worship, "He is risen," but it came out in a flat monotone, and the sermon on the resurrection that followed was lifeless. Virginia and I laugh about it now, but at the time I knew I was doing the church a disservice. I repented. It was a wake-up call to reassess my work, the way I

---

3    Herbert J. Freudenberger, *Burn-Out: The High Cost of High Achievement* (New York: Doubleday, 1980), 13.

was doing it, and the pressure I was placing on myself. I realized in a fresh way that faithfulness in pastoral ministry was not a quick sprint to please others or myself, but a long-distance marathon that was impossible to run without fixing my eyes on Jesus. About this time a pastor, who was also a friend, preached on what to do when you hit the wall. He turned to the burned-out prophet Elijah. On the run from his enemies and himself, Elijah sat down under the scant shade of the broom tree and prayed that he might die. "I have had enough, LORD," he said. "Take my life; I am no better than my ancestors" (1 Kings 19:4). I'd say that it is easier for most pastors to picture themselves under the broom tree bemoaning their spiritual weakness and failure than it is for them to declare victory over false prophets and idolatry on top of Mount Carmel. Like Elijah, we are haunted by feelings of failure. What the Lord did next for Elijah reveals a pattern of renewal that remains essential for pastors today. God strengthened his body, restored his soul, and renewed his calling.

Food and rest were all that his body needed, but his soul required a long slow journey to Horeb. Elijah's ten-day trip turned into forty days and forty nights, a journey reminiscent of Israel's forty years in the wilderness and Moses's forty days on Mount Sinai. Elijah's trek foreshadowed Jesus's forty days in the wilderness. In Jewish custom, a period of mourning lasts forty days. Perhaps, it took that long for Elijah to accept the fact that spiritual renewal was not going to sweep Israel as he had hoped and prayed. The Lord gave Elijah the time and space to mourn Israel's apostasy.

When the prophet reached Horeb, the Lord asked him, "'What are you doing here, Elijah?'" (1 Kings 19:9). The question is best interpreted as a comforting reminder rather than a rebuke. Elijah was encouraged to face his feelings, examine his motives, and reassess his situation. He answered the question by reviewing his ministry: "'I have been very zealous for the LORD God Almighty. The Israelites have rejected your covenant, torn down your altars, and put your prophets to death with the sword. I am the only one left, and now they are trying to kill me too'" (1 Kings 19:10). The

Lord replied, "'Go out and stand on the mountain in the presence of the LORD, for the LORD is about to pass by'" (1 Kings 19:11). The Lord was not in the wind or earthquake or fire, but in a gentle whisper. The Lord then asked Elijah, a second time, why he was there. The prophet repeated his answer word for word. He felt the same zeal for the Lord that he had always felt, but in the wake of Israel's hardhearted indifference and apostasy he felt alone and helpless. Instead of giving Elijah easy answers, the Lord recommissioned him. He reminded Elijah of his larger purpose. He ordered Elijah to anoint God's instruments of judgment—the new kings of Aram and Israel—and a new prophet, Elisha. Then, the Lord informed him that there were seven thousand devoted followers of the Lord God who had not bowed down to Baal (1 Kings 19:18). Elijah may have felt alone, but he was not. The Lord refocused Elijah and renewed his sense of communion and community. He gave him a vision for faithfulness to the end. As the years go by, all pastors periodically need the renewal that Elijah needed and experienced.

## NO HEROES, ONLY MENTORS

I love the way the apostle John describes his pastoral identity: "I, John, your brother and companion in the suffering and kingdom and patient endurance that are ours in Jesus, was on the island of Patmos because of the word of God and the testimony of Jesus" (Rev. 1:9). John impresses me as the kind of mentor I can learn from, and throughout my ministry I have had individuals, like John, who ministered to me in that way. As that passage continues, John uses the first-person singular "I" seven times, but always in relation to the action of God (see Rev. 1:9–17). His sevenfold self-description encompasses his personal identity and redemptive story. He is our brother in the family of God. His individual "I" does not stand alone. Whether he was by himself on the island of Patmos, exiled and physically removed frrom the seven churches, or in the company of other Christians, he was never alone. Rather, in the Spirit, he remained a companion to the fellowship of believers in the "suffering and kingdom and patient endurance that are ours in Jesus." All three attributes of companionship—the suffering and kingdom and patient endurance—are inseparable and stand together. John's self-description underscores the priesthood of all believers: "To him who loves us and has freed us from our sins by his blood, and has made us to be a kingdom and priests to serve his God and Father—to him be glory and power for ever and ever! Amen" (Rev. 1:5–6).

Like John, we want to be where we are because of "the word of God and the testimony of Jesus Christ" (Rev. 1:2). Neither Caesar nor his modern equivalents determine our response to our circumstances; the Lord and his Word do. John was not on Rome's watch list because he was an outspoken critic of Rome, but because he proclaimed ultimate fidelity and loyalty to the imminent return of the true King of kings and Lord of lords. Jesus is Lord, not Caesar. John's personal experience of this ever-deepening crisis of history was due to the Word of God and the testimony of Jesus. "Wherever the gospel is preached," writes Lesslie Newbigin, whenever the gospel and the community formed by the gospel raise the question of ultimate meaning, "new ideologies appear—secular humanism, nationalism, Marxism." These "other messiahs," Newbigin writes, promise their version of freedom "from all the ills that beset human life." And so, "the crisis of history is deepened."[4]

Into the deepening crisis of history, the Lord continues to send his people, but there are no heroes, only saints who have gone before. Faithfulness to the end runs contrary to cultural expectations: No memorials. No shrines. No celebrities. The Bible does not enshrine the patriarchs, prophets, and apostles. Their graves might as well be unmarked. They are remembered, but not lionized, much less idolized. They come and go quietly without fanfare and a praise band. Their lives are engulfed by the big picture of salvation. That's all they could think about, and that's all God wants us to think about. Since God saw fit to reveal his Word without artistic

---

4    Leslie Newbigin, *The Gospel in a Pluralistic Society* (Grand Rapids: Eerdmans, 1989), 122.

sketches of the prophets and the apostles, we have no idea what these key figures in salvation history even looked like. No tombs to visit. No pictures to honor. The Bible's absolute indifference to images and appearance curbs our appetite for hero worship and starves our bent toward personality cults and idolatry.[5] The tide of salvation history moves out, we pass from the scene, and a new generation of saints moves in.

John guides us in how to live for Christ in an anti-Christian world. The challenge is as simple as it is difficult. He writes, "This calls for patient endurance and faithfulness on the part of God's people" (Rev. 13:10; see also 14:12). John has nothing new to add. We have heard it all before. Keep God's commandments and hold fast to the testimony about Jesus. Remain pure and undefiled (Rev. 12:17). Follow the Lamb; speak the truth (14:4–5). Stay alert. Be ready at a moment's notice. It's what the saints have always done: prayer and obedience, worship and witness, purity and truth-telling. To be faithful requires wisdom and the ability to discern the true nature of evil. Confidence resides not in our own personal stamina or will power, but in God's faithfulness.

When we came to First Presbyterian Church of San Diego in 1993 our children were young, and I was a young pastor. Little did we or the church know what this undertaking would involve. Together, as a church, we embarked on what became a fourteen-year journey. Along the way, we faced plenty of challenges, a painful split over same-sex unions, internal conflicts over church growth, poor staffing decisions, and so on. We also experienced plenty of opportunities. We welcomed many new Christians into the kingdom. We saw families thrive in Christ, and we witnessed the courage of those in our congregation who suffered for Christ. Some of the best sermons preached in our church were not from the pulpit, but by our brothers and sisters in Christ from the perspective of their difficult life circumstances. When we moved from the church to the seminary, I wrote:

---

5   See Webster, *Living in Tension*, 2:201.

You have made me a better pastor and backed me with prayer and generous support. The church has encouraged my mission trips and challenged me to preach more effectively. You have embraced the biblical vision of the household of faith and studied the Word of God for yourselves. Many of you have assumed responsibilities in the church and served one another with the fruit and gifts of the Spirit. You have cared for the needy, fed the homeless, educated the young, supported global missions, worshiped the Lord faithfully, and sought to honor Christ in all that you do. I am most grateful for this time as your pastor. . . .

I dread saying goodbye to this household of faith. You have been on my mind and in my heart nonstop for fourteen years of my prime working life.

## FOREVER YOUNG

Søren Kierkegaard writes, "Don't finish with life until it's finished with you."[6] Kierkegaard reasoned that life is not like a school exam that we can finish ahead of time if we are especially clever. Life doesn't work that way. We can't retire early from a life of faith in Christ any more than we can retire early from life itself. As Yankee baseball legend Yogi Berra famously said, "It's not over until it's over."

I have five young grandchildren. When I'm with adults, I *know* I am a child of God, but when I'm with my grandkids I *feel* like a child of God. My grandkids are parables reminding me of my dependence upon my heavenly Father. I'm sure I don't impress the Lord the way my grandkids impress me, but when I'm with them, watching over them, making sure nothing happens to them, and

---

6    Sorén Kierkegaard, *Parables of Kierkegaard*, ed. Thomas C. Oden (Princeton, NJ: Princeton University Press, 1989), 85.

playing with them, I sense the Lord watching over me too. I know that the Lord cares for me and loves me to a degree far deeper than even my love for my family.

There is a wonderful corollary to growing old in Christ. The older I am in Christ the younger I become. As the weight of physical ailments and the world's worries grow heavier, my spirit grows lighter. We get better at casting all our anxiety on the Lord, knowing that he cares for us (1 Peter 5:7). We can afford to feel, with the apostle Paul, some sense of satisfaction: "I have fought the good fight, I have finished the race, I have kept the faith" (2 Tim. 4:7). Instead of worrying about a legacy, we acknowledge our dependence upon the Lord. When we look back, it is not to measure accomplishments, but to the thank the Lord for his provision and protection. We know that life is measured not by what we have achieved, but by what we have received.

Hans Urs von Balthasar claims Christ is the model for deep maturity and childlike intimacy:

> And the more we identify ourselves with the mission entrusted to us, in the manner of the eternal Son, the more thoroughly do we become sons and daughters of the Heavenly Father: the whole Sermon on the Mount testifies to this. In the figures of the great saints the truth is crystal clear: Christian childlikeness and Christian maturity are not in tension with one another. Even at an advanced age, the saints enjoy a marvelous youthfulness.[7]

Augustine's response to the psalmist's plea to God, "Do not cast me away when I am old; do not forsake me when my strength is gone," is bold (Ps. 71:9). He is up for the challenge. He says in effect, "Bring it on! Go ahead let your strength fail, in order that you may abide in the strength of God and learn to say with the apostle, 'For

---

7    Hans Urs von Balthhasar, *Unless You Become Like This Child* (San Francisco: Ignatius, 1991), 41.

when I am weak, then I am strong' (2 Cor. 12:10)." But Augustine also insists we remember Isaiah's words, "He gives strength to the weary and increases the power of the weak. Even youths grow tired and weary, and young men stumble and fall; but those who hope in the LORD will renew their strength. They will soar on wings like eagles; they will run and not grow weary, they will walk and not be faint" (Isa. 40:29–31).[8]

---

8    Augustine, "Expositions on the Book of Psalms," ed. Philip Schaff, trans. A. Cleveland Coxe, vol. 8 in *Nicene and Post-Nicene Fathers* (Peabody, MA: Hendrickson, 1995), 318.

# OTHER TITLES
# BY THE AUTHOR

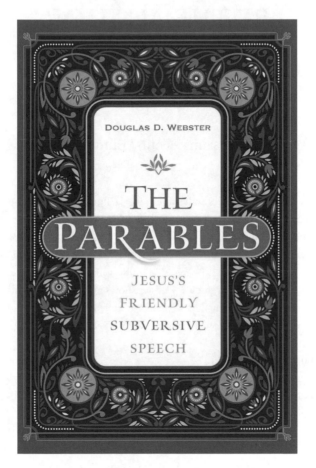

## The Parables: Jesus's Friendly Subversive Speech
ISBN: 9780825446900

Jesus's parables used familiar situations to convey deep spiritual truths in ways that are provocative and subversive of the status quo. Prayerfulness was pictured by a persistent widow. The joy of salvation in the homecoming of a lost son. Love of neighbor by a marginalized Samaritan. If we're not careful, we can easily miss details in the parables that reveal their subtle meanings as well as their contemporary relevance.

# OTHER TITLES
# BY THE AUTHOR

## The Psalms - Four-Volume Set
ISBN: 9780825447556

The Old Testament Psalter testifies both to the universal human condition and the redemption wrought for believers in the person and work of Christ. In The Psalms: Jesus's Prayer Book, longtime pastor and seminary professor Doug Webster distills ancient and modern scholarship on the Psalms into theological, canonical, apostolic, linguistic, and pastoral edification to students of Psalter. By focusing on both the most consequential and the less developed aspects of Psalm studies, Webster shows how living a Christ-centered life goes hand in hand with digesting the Psalms as a complete collection prefiguring Christ. The volumes of The Psalms follow the internal divisions Psalms presents:

Volume 1 (Book I of the Psalms)
Volume 2 (Book II)
Volume 3 (Book III-IV)
Volume 4 (Book V)

Designed with preachers and teachers in mind, The Psalms strikes a middle ground between a technical commentary and a book of sermons. Webster offers pastoral insight in both interpretation and application of the Psalms for worship, unveiling purpose and significance for worship, devotion, and reflection.

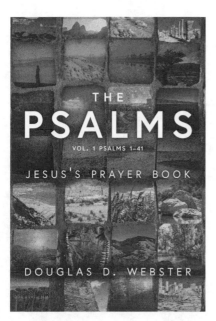

THE
PSALMS
VOL. 1 PSALMS 1–41
JESUS'S PRAYER BOOK
DOUGLAS D. WEBSTER

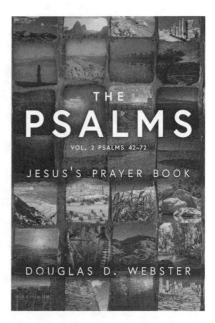

THE
PSALMS
VOL. 2 PSALMS 42–72
JESUS'S PRAYER BOOK
DOUGLAS D. WEBSTER

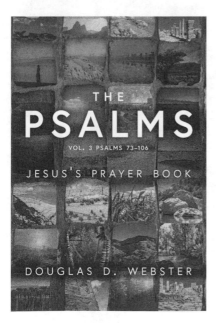

THE
PSALMS
VOL. 3 PSALMS 73–106
JESUS'S PRAYER BOOK
DOUGLAS D. WEBSTER

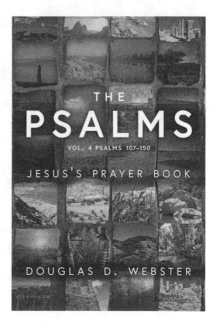

THE
PSALMS
VOL. 4 PSALMS 107–150
JESUS'S PRAYER BOOK
DOUGLAS D. WEBSTER